Strength Training for Women Over 40:
Dumbbell Edition

Build Muscle, Transform Your Body, and Boost Confidence with Quick and Effective Exercises

21-day At-Home
Dumbbell workout!

Thank you for buying my book!
As a small token of my gratitude,
here is a Quick Guide to Injury Prevention for Women Over 40.
Just take a picture of the QR code with your phone,
and you will receive the free PDF!

If you want to connect with me, find me at:

amynealcoaching.com

or on Facebook at:

Amy Neal Coaching

Dedication:

I dedicate this book to my daughters, *Cana and Malina*.
You both are teenagers right now,
but I hope you know every part of this book is for you.
I love you both with my whole heart.
Thanks for all our adventures and for letting my love
for strength and fitness seep into your life.
You both make me want to be a better woman
and mom every single day.
"The Joy of the Lord is my Strength"

Table of Contents:

Introduction

Hi there! I'm so happy you grabbed this book! If you've read any of my books by now, you know how passionate I am about strength training! It's life-changing, especially for women over 40! Lifting weights provides so much more than just building and strengthening your muscles. It gives you more energy, increases confidence, and makes you feel incredibly powerful.

This book is all about dumbbell workouts. I created this book to show women how versatile and efficient dumbbells are. You can do a variety of exercises with them, and they're great for beginners and seasoned fitness enthusiasts. Plus, you don't need a lot of space for these workouts. You could do these exercises in your living room, bedroom, or backyard!

I've been a Certified Personal Trainer since 2003 and a Certified Nutrition Coach since 2020. I've helped people from all walks of life reach their fitness goals, and now I'm here to help you!

You can read about fitness all you want, but change will only come when you commit to putting into practice what you have read in these pages. Your body is truly capable of so much! There's nothing quite like seeing the positive changes in your body, feeling stronger, healthier, and more confident.

This book is about more than just working out. I want to help you create a lifestyle that makes you feel great about yourself!

Let me tell you a little bit about myself!

I'm Amy, and as I said above, I've been a fitness professional since 2003. I've coached and trained all ages, genders, sizes, and fitness levels for over 20 years. I am a Certified Personal Trainer through the National Academy of Sports Medicine (NASM), holding certifications in Balance and Training Movements and Behavioral Change Specialist with NASM. I am also a Certified Nutrition Coach through Precision Nutrition. I have held other certifications in my long career through ISSA and CrossFit.

On a personal level, strength training has been life-changing for me. I started lifting weights in High School but fell in love with it during my years of training and coaching CrossFit. The confidence I gained through lifting weights is extraordinary, and the joy I get from being strong and using my muscles is unexplainable.

My true joy is to meet anyone on any level in their health journey. Whether you are getting back to fitness or a beginner hesitant to start, I want to walk the road with you!

Teaching people about strength training is a joy and passion of mine, and I can't wait to teach you about the effective workouts you can gain from Dumbbells alone!

Chapter 1:
The Female Body
and Strength Training

I can't tell you how often I've heard a woman say, "I don't want to lift weights because it will make me look bulky." That's why I'm here, typing away on my keyboard, trying to debunk some of the most prevalent myths associated with strength training for women. You're not alone if you've found yourself holding onto these misconceptions. So, let's get to the truth about lifting weights for women!

1.1 Debunking Strength Training Myths

Myth 1: Strength Training Makes Women Bulky

'Strength Training Makes Women Bulky' is probably the most common fear that keeps women from picking up those dumbbells. But here's the truth - women naturally have less muscle tissue and produce lower levels of testosterone than men. Testosterone plays a significant role in muscle development. So, even with the same amount of strength training as men, women will not become bodybuilders overnight.

Instead, strength training helps us develop lean muscle tissue that makes us stronger, helps us burn calories more efficiently, and makes our muscles strong and evident in our bodies! You're creating a strong, capable body that can carry groceries up two flights of stairs, lift your kids, or hold a plank for a minute straight.

Myth 2: Cardio is the Only Way to Lose Weight

While cardio is essential to a balanced fitness routine, it's not the only way to lose weight.

Strength training can be a more effective weight loss strategy. Strength training builds more muscle than cardio, and muscle is a metabolically active tissue, meaning it burns calories even when you're at rest. So, the more muscle you have, the more calories you burn throughout the day, not just during your workout. It's like having a little calorie-burning machine inside you.

Myth 3: Lifting Heavy Weights is Dangerous for Women

Just like in any physical activity, the risk of injury in strength training lies in improper form, not the activity itself. Lifting heavy weights is not inherently dangerous for women. The key is learning the correct technique before adding heavy weights.

Start with lighter weights, get the form right, and gradually increase the weight as your strength improves. Always listen to your body and never push through pain. If something doesn't feel right, it isn't.

Strength training is not a "no pain, no gain" scenario. It's important to gradually challenge your body, increase your strength, and care for yourself. Lifting weights is no more dangerous for women than it is for men.

Remember, every body is unique. What works for one may not work for another. Listen to your body, respect its limits, and celebrate its capabilities.

You're stronger than you think. And with the correct training and proper movement, you can be even stronger.

1.2 Benefits of Strength Training for Women

Let's talk about the benefits of strength training for women! The benefits are numerous, but let's dive into some of the most significant ones.

Improved Bone Health

First, we have improved bone health. Did you know that women are more susceptible to bone-related conditions like osteoporosis than men, particularly as we age? It's true. The good news is that strength training can help counteract this.

When you lift weights, you're not just working your muscles. You're also putting a healthy sort of stress on your bones. This stress signals your body to bolster bone density, which can help ward off osteoporosis and other bone health issues. It's like a protective shield for your skeleton, making it stronger and more resilient.

Elevated Mood and Energy Levels

Next is something we could all use a little more of – energy and a positive mood. Strength training is a natural mood booster. It stimulates the production of endorphins, those feel-good hormones that make you happier and more upbeat.

Maybe you're having a rough day - you're swamped with work, the kids are making you a bit crazy, or you're just feeling down. You pick up your dumbbells and start your workout. By the end of the session, you feel like a weight has been lifted off your shoulders (pun intended). That's the power of endorphins in a workout!

And it's not just about feeling good. Regular strength training can also help you feel more energetic and alert. You might feel tired immediately after a workout, but consistent strength training can significantly improve your energy levels.

Increased Metabolic Rate

Lastly, we've got a boosted metabolic rate. Your metabolic rate is the speed at which your body burns calories. As we mentioned earlier, muscle tissue is metabolically active, meaning the more muscle you have, the more calories you burn, even when you're not working out.

By engaging in strength training and building muscle, you're essentially turning your body into a more efficient calorie-burning machine.

The benefits of improved bone health, elevated mood and energy levels, and a revved-up metabolic rate are just scratching the surface. A whole host of other benefits come with strength training, from improved posture and better balance to increased physical strength and endurance.

1.3 The Role of Hormones in Muscle Growth

Now we know the fantastic benefits of strength training on our bodies. Let's dig a bit deeper into the science behind muscle growth. I promise not to turn this into a dry, tedious biology lecture! Think of it more as a behind-the-scenes tour of your body, which is pretty fascinating.

Estrogen and Muscle Repair

First, let's talk about estrogen. The very hormone defines us as women and plays a significant role in muscle repair. When lifting weights, you create tiny tears in your muscle fibers, which is a normal part of the strength training process. Estrogen steps in to help repair these micro-tears, rebuilding the muscle fibers to be stronger and more resilient.

Growth Hormone and Muscle Development

Next, we have the growth hormone. When released into the bloodstream, this hormone stimulates muscle growth, helps to metabolize fat, and improves bone density. When you get a good night's sleep or engage in high-intensity workouts, your body naturally secretes more of this growth hormone.

Lifting weights does so much more than build muscle. It triggers a whole cascade of events in your body that contribute to your overall health and well-being. I think it's pretty amazing!

Insulin's Role in Muscle Growth

Last, let us talk about insulin. Now, insulin often gets a bad rap, primarily because of its association with diabetes. But insulin is crucial for muscle growth. It acts like a key, unlocking your cells to absorb the sugar from your blood and use it for energy.

Your blood sugar rises when you eat a meal, especially one rich in carbohydrates. Your pancreas then releases insulin to help your cells absorb this sugar. If you've just done a strength training workout, your muscles are primed to absorb and use this sugar to repair and grow.

So, insulin fuels your muscles, helping them recover after a workout and grow stronger. But remember, balance is key. You want to feed your muscles with nutritious, whole foods that provide a steady release of energy rather than spiking your blood sugar levels with processed, sugary snacks.

Your body is an incredible machine. It's constantly working, repairing, growing, and adapting. Strength training gives your body the tools to become stronger, healthier, and more resilient. Strength training helps you look good, and it also helps nurture and care for your body so you can live your best life.

1.4 Understanding Body Composition

Let's talk about body composition. You might have heard this term buzzing around fitness circles, but what does it mean? Body composition refers to everything your body comprises: fat mass and fat-free mass. Fat-free mass includes muscles, bones, water, and organs.

The Difference Between Body Weight and Body Fat Percentage

Body weight differs from body fat percentage. Body weight includes muscles, bones, water, organs, and fat. However, body fat percentage is the proportion of your weight that's made up of fat.

Consider this: you have two individuals who both weigh 150 pounds. One has a body fat percentage of 20%, while the other has a body fat percentage of 30%. Even though they weigh the same, the person with a higher body fat percentage has more fat and less muscle. On the other hand, the person with a lower body fat percentage has less fat and more muscle.

So, when tracking your progress, don't just rely on the number on the scale. It only tells part of the story.

Importance of Lean Muscle Mass

Why is muscle mass so significant? Muscles are your body's powerhouses. They keep you strong, help you move, and boost your metabolism. Remember how we talked about muscle being metabolically active? That's why a body with muscle burns more calories, even at rest.

Having a higher percentage of muscle mass also means you have a lower percentage of fat mass, which is linked to a lower risk of certain health conditions like heart disease, diabetes, and high blood pressure. So, by building muscle through strength training, you're not just building a strong body but also contributing to your overall health.

How Strength Training Affects Body Composition

How does strength training tie into all this? When you lift weights, you create micro-tears in your muscles. Your body then repairs these tears, building your muscles stronger and bigger, increasing your muscle mass, boosting your metabolism, and helping you burn more calories.

At the same time, strength training can also help you lose fat. When you perform strength training exercises, your body taps into your fat stores for energy. This, combined with a healthy diet, can help you decrease your body fat percentage.

Strength training can help you build muscle and lose fat, improving your body composition. But remember, changes in body composition don't happen overnight. It takes consistency, patience, and a healthy relationship with food and exercise. We are focusing on long-term, healthy habits, not quick fixes that aren't sustainable over time.

Chapter 2:
The Miracle of Muscle

Our muscles are constantly working, contracting, and relaxing, enabling us to move, breathe, and even blink!

Muscles are a marvel of human biology, but they're not just there to help us lift heavy objects or show off our strong, toned arms in sleeveless dresses. They're essential for our overall health and wellness. When we engage in strength training, we initiate physiological changes in our muscles, leading to increased strength and size, a process known as muscle hypertrophy.

2.1 The Science Behind Muscle Growth

The Process of Muscle Hypertrophy

Muscle hypertrophy sounds complex, but it's really straightforward once you break it down. 'Hyper' means over or more, and 'trophy' means growth. So, muscle hypertrophy simply means the growth and increase of the size of muscle cells.

The weights you lift place a load on your muscles that they're not used to, causing tiny, microscopic tears in the muscle fibers. Your body then repairs these tears, and in the process, the muscle fibers grow larger and stronger.

How Resistance Training Stimulates Muscle Growth

Resistance training (like lifting dumbbells) is the stimulus your muscles need to start the repair and growth process. It's like sending a signal to your body saying, "Hey, we need to be stronger to handle this load."

Your body responds by increasing the production of certain types of cells called satellite cells. Think of these as little helpers that rush to the damaged site and assist in the repair process. They fuse to the damaged muscle fibers, increasing their size and adding new proteins, leading to muscle growth.

But remember, this doesn't happen while you're lifting the weights. The growth and repair process occurs when resting, especially when sleeping. That's why rest days and adequate sleep are crucial for muscle growth.

The Role of Nutrition in Muscle Development

Your body needs fuel to repair and build muscles. Fueling your muscles is where nutrition comes into play.

Protein is one of the most important nutrients for muscle growth. It's the building blocks of your muscles. When you consume protein, your body breaks it down into amino acids, which are used to repair the damaged muscle fibers and build new ones.

Carbohydrates also play an important role in muscle development. They provide the energy your body needs to perform the workouts and function optimally.

While it's important to consume enough protein and carbohydrates, it's also essential to maintain a balanced diet with enough fruits, vegetables, healthy fats, and hydration. Your body needs various nutrients to function at its best.

So, the next time you pick up those dumbbells, remember, you're not just working out. You're triggering a remarkable chain of events, a whole domino effect of biological processes, all aimed at making you stronger, healthier, and more capable!

In the following sections, we'll further explore the fascinating world of muscles, delving into how age affects muscle mass, the importance of muscle for overall health, and how to balance strength training and cardio in your workout routine. I can't wait for you to gain a newfound appreciation for your muscles and all the incredible things they allow you to do!

2.2 How Age Affects Muscle Mass

Let's talk about something we all experience, but only some talk about - aging. Now, don't get me wrong. Aging has its perks: wisdom, knowledge, and a well-earned sense of self-confidence. But let's face it, it also comes with a few challenges. One of those challenges is muscle loss. Just as the color of our hair changes over time, so does our muscle mass. It's a natural part of aging, but we can slow down the process and maintain our strength and vitality with the right tools and knowledge.

The Phenomenon of Sarcopenia

The technical term for age-related muscle loss is sarcopenia, from the Greek words 'sarx' meaning flesh, and 'penia' meaning reduction. Starting as early as our 30s, we can lose 3-5% of our muscle mass each decade. By the time we hit our seventies, this loss can accelerate, impacting our strength, balance, and overall quality of life.

But here's the thing: While sarcopenia is a natural part of aging, it's not inevitable. Just as a well-maintained car can run smoothly for many years, so can our bodies. And strength training can help us do this.

How Strength Training Can Combat Age-Related Muscle Loss

Strength training is the magic potion for aging muscles. It helps stimulate the production of muscle proteins, slow down muscle loss, and even build new muscle. Lifting weights puts a healthy strain on our muscles, signaling them to grow stronger and more resilient.

This is my favorite example: I told you earlier how I have trained people of all ages of life with weight training. Some of my favorite clients are my 76-year-old parents! I have been training them 2-3 times a week for over six years. They don't have huge muscles, but their bodies don't resemble your average 76-year-old. They move well and have energy; you can see muscle in their bodies! Essentially, we are slowing their aging process by maintaining their muscle mass and slowing down their muscle loss. Even more than looks, their yearly bloodwork is always great, and when they see their doctors for regular checkups, they can't believe they are 76 years old. I would say they look and move more like they are in their mid-60s! It's incredible!

The Importance of Protein Intake as We Age

Our muscles need to get the right nutrients to grow and repair. The most critical nutrient for muscle repair and growth is protein.

Proteins are made up of amino acids, the building blocks of our muscles. When we consume protein, our body breaks it down into these amino acids, which are then used to repair and build new muscle fibers.

As we age, our muscles become less efficient at using these amino acids, which means we might need more protein in our diet than when we were younger.

But remember, not all proteins are created equal. Aim for high-quality protein sources like lean meats, fish, eggs, and dairy, as well as plant-based options like legumes, nuts, and seeds. These provide all the essential amino acids your muscles need to repair and grow.

So, while we can't stop the clock, we can influence how our bodies change as we age. Consistent strength training and a diet rich in high-quality protein can slow down muscle loss, maintain our strength, and help us enjoy an active, vibrant life at any age.

Our muscles are amazing! They support us, help us move, and even boost our mood.

2.3 The Importance of Muscle for Overall Health

Muscles contribute to our overall health in remarkable ways. Let's explore how muscles influence metabolism, balance, mobility, and heart health.

Muscle's role in metabolism and weight management

Did you ever wonder why some people seem to eat all they want and never gain an ounce, while others have to watch every calorie? The answer lies in our metabolism - the rate at which our bodies burn calories. And guess what? Muscles, being the metabolic powerhouses they are, play a crucial role in this process.

Muscle tissue is metabolically active, which burns calories even when you're not working out. The more muscle mass you have, the higher your resting metabolic rate. That's why strength training, which helps build muscle, can be a powerful ally in weight management.

So, while lifting dumbbells might seem like a simple physical activity, it's sparking a metabolic revolution inside your body, helping you burn more calories and manage your weight more effectively.

How muscle mass affects balance and mobility

Imagine walking on a tightrope. You'd need an incredible sense of balance, right? Think about everyday activities like climbing stairs, reaching a high shelf, or even walking on uneven surfaces. They all require balance too, don't they? And guess what helps us maintain this balance and mobility? That's right, it's our muscles.

Muscles work together in perfect harmony to keep us upright and moving smoothly. They support our joints and help us navigate a world full of physical challenges, from icy sidewalks to crowded dance floors.

Strength training helps improve our balance and mobility by building stronger, more efficient muscles. This can minimize the risk of falls and injuries, especially as we age. So, every bicep curl, every squat, every deadlift is helping you move through life with greater ease and confidence.

The link between muscle strength and cardiovascular health

Now, let's get to the heart of the matter. The link between muscle strength and cardiovascular health may not be obvious, but it's incredibly significant.

You're not just working your muscles when you engage in strength training. You're also giving your heart a fantastic workout. As you lift those dumbbells, your heart rate increases, improving circulation and delivering more oxygen to your hardworking muscles. Over time, this can lower your resting heart rate and blood pressure, reducing the risk of heart disease.

But that's not all. Muscles, especially the large ones in your legs and back, are crucial in maintaining healthy cholesterol levels. When these muscles contract, they signal your body to take up more 'bad' cholesterol from your blood and transport it to your liver to be broken down.

So, the next time you lift those dumbbells, remember that you're not just strengthening your muscles but also taking care of your heart in the most active way possible.

Muscles contribute to our overall health in more ways than one. They help us burn calories, maintain balance and mobility, and even protect our heart health. We can nurture and strengthen these muscles right in the comfort of our homes with just a pair of dumbbells!

If you want to go straight to the Dumbbell Movements, head over to Chapter 4!

2.4 Strength Training vs Cardio: Balancing Your Workout Routine

The perfect workout combo offers strength, stamina, flexibility, and an endorphin-infused glow that makes you feel invincible! But it's hard for some people to devise a good workout program to accomplish all those fantastic outcomes, and it is overwhelming for most people I know!

In the next part of this chapter, I will introduce you to a balanced workout routine that includes strength training and cardio—a powerful combination that can help you achieve your fitness goals.

The Benefits of Combining Cardio and Strength Training

Each type of exercise (Cardio and Strength Training) contributes different benefits to your overall fitness.

As we've discussed, strength training provides a strong foundation. It helps build muscle, boost metabolism, and improve bone density. Cardio increases your heart rate, improves lung capacity, and boosts your endurance.

When you combine strength training and cardio, you get a full-body workout that helps you build muscle and burn fat, improves your heart health, and boosts your stamina.

How to Incorporate Both into Your Workout Routine

Let's discuss how to strike the right balance between cardio and strength training in your workout routine. A common approach is to alternate between cardio and strength training days. This gives your muscles ample time to rest and recover after strength training while keeping your heart rate up with cardio.

Alternatively, you could also do both on the same day. Start with a strength training session and then finish with a quick cardio workout. This way, you're effectively hitting two birds with one stone. You're challenging your muscles with strength training and then using cardio to burn even more calories.

Remember, listening to your body and adapting your routine as needed is key. Some days, you might be up for a high-intensity strength training session followed by cardio. On other days, a low-intensity cardio workout might be all you need. Each day is different, and that's perfectly okay. Fitness is not one-size-fits-all; it's a customized journey.

As of writing this book, my workouts look like this:

- Monday: Strength - Deadlift and Power Cleans. 30-minute run, medium intensity.

- Tuesday: Strength - Shoulders and Arms, finish with a 10-minute HIIT workout.

- Wednesday: Strength - Squats. Go for a walk later in the day.

- Thursday: Active recovery - go for an hour's walk or a jog and stretch. Or, some Thursdays, I do nothing!

- Friday: Strength - Chest and Back. Go for a walk later in the day.

- Saturday: Long run (or walk, depending on how I feel!)

This combination has worked well for me. My focus is always on Strength, but I get my heart moving on my runs and walks. I feel strong and ready for any fun activity thrown my way! As a 46-year-old woman, I still feel like I'm in my 20s! (I get tired at 9 pm now!)

Remember that this is my fitness road. I have been lifting heavy weights, hard since 2012. I spent years working on movement patterns with coaches and getting certified in those movements. I've had years to build my fitness base, and my capacity is pretty high because of the years I have put in. This workout schedule has a much lower capacity than when I participated in CrossFit for 15 years, but it is sustainable. I could do this schedule for a long time!

The Concept of Active Rest and Cross-Training

Have you ever heard of the phrase 'active rest'? It might sound like an oxymoron, but it's crucial to fitness. Active rest days are when you engage in low-intensity activities like walking, stretching, or yoga. These activities help your muscles recover while keeping your body moving.

On the other hand, cross-training involves engaging in different types of exercises to give certain muscle groups a break while working others. This not only helps prevent overuse injuries but also keeps your workouts exciting and diverse.

For example, if you've been doing a lot of lower-body strength training, you might opt for an upper-body-focused activity like swimming on your cross-training days. This way, you're giving your legs a rest while still working your upper body.

In the end, remember that fitness is not a race; it's a lifelong commitment to your health. Balancing strength training and cardio is about creating a routine that challenges you, keeps you motivated, and, most importantly, is something you enjoy. After all, the best workout is the one you'll stick with.

Chapter 3:
The Power of Dumbbells:
Compact, Versatile, and Effective

Dumbbells aren't flashy or intricate. They're simple, compact, and incredibly versatile. And they offer everything you need for a comprehensive workout right within your grasp. Welcome to chapter three, where we explore the versatility, balanced muscle development, and convenience of at-home workouts with dumbbells!

3.1 Why Dumbbells?

The Versatility of Dumbbell Exercises

Using a dumbbell for workouts opens up a multitude of exercises. From bicep curls and tricep extensions to lunges and squats, there's a dumbbell exercise for every major muscle group in your body.

Think about a typical day. You're lifting grocery bags (hello, bicep curls), picking up your child or your pet (yup, that's a squat), or reaching overhead to grab something from a high shelf (overhead press!). Dumbbell exercises often mimic everyday movements, making them functional and practical.

But the versatility of dumbbells doesn't stop there. You can easily adjust the intensity of your workouts by changing the weight of the dumbbells. Starting with light dumbbells and gradually increasing the weight as you get stronger allows for progressive overload, a critical factor in muscle growth and strength development.

Dumbbells Promote Balanced Muscle Development

Remember the last time you tried to carry an overloaded shopping bag in one hand? It felt awkward and unbalanced, right? That's because our bodies crave symmetry and balance. And guess what? Dumbbells can help achieve just that.

When you use dumbbells, you engage both sides of your body equally, which ensures balanced muscle development and prevents muscular imbalances that can lead to posture issues or injuries. For instance, when you perform a bicep curl with a dumbbell in each hand, they lift an equal load, promoting symmetrical muscle growth.

Moreover, dumbbells engage not just your primary muscles but also your stabilizing muscles. These muscles help maintain proper form and control while lifting weights. For example, during a dumbbell overhead press, your core muscles come into play, helping keep your body stable as you lift the weights above your head. This total body engagement results in a more effective and balanced workout.

The Convenience of At-Home Workouts with Dumbbells

There's something incredibly liberating about working out at home! No more rushing to the gym during peak hours, waiting for your turn at the weight rack, or wiping down sweaty equipment. You can create your fitness sanctuary right at home with a pair of dumbbells.

Dumbbells are compact and easy to store, requiring little space, making them perfect for home workouts. Whether in your living room, backyard, or bedroom, you can have a full-body strength training session with your dumbbells.

And it's not just about convenience. Working out at home allows you to experiment, make mistakes, and learn at your own pace. You can blast your favorite music, wear whatever you want, and take breaks when you need to. You can create a workout environment where you feel comfortable and empowered.

Dumbbells are like the Swiss army knife of fitness equipment. They're versatile, promote balanced muscle development, and are convenient for at-home workouts. Whether you're a fitness newbie or a seasoned pro, dumbbells offer an effective and efficient way to strength train. They can help make fitness a seamless part of your life rather than something you have to fit into your schedule.

3.2 Types of Dumbbells: Your Tools to Transformation

So, you're ready to incorporate strength training into your fitness routine, and dumbbells are your equipment of choice. You'll find that dumbbells come in different types, each with unique features that cater to various fitness levels, preferences, and budgets. Let's explore the world of fixed-weight dumbbells, adjustable dumbbells, and hex dumbbells.

Fixed Weight Dumbbells: A Classic Choice

Do you recall seeing those shiny, color-coded weights lined up on a rack at the gym? Those are fixed-weight dumbbells. As the name suggests, the weight of these dumbbells is fixed, meaning you can't add or remove weights. Each dumbbell is a different weight, ranging from light to heavy.

Fixed-weight dumbbells are a classic choice. They're simple, straightforward, and easy to use. You just pick up the weight you want and get to work. There's no fussing around with changing weights or worrying about loose plates. It's just you and the dumbbell, ready to conquer your workout.

These dumbbells are great if you're doing a workout that requires switching between different weights quickly. Think of a high-intensity interval training (HIIT) workout where you're alternating between lighter weights for cardio moves and heavier weights for strength exercises.

Adjustable Dumbbells: The All in One Solution

Next up, we have adjustable dumbbells. Picture a compact, space-saving workout station that offers a whole range of weights, all within a single dumbbell. That's exactly what adjustable dumbbells are.

These dumbbells come with weight plates you can add or remove to adjust the weight. They are a full set of dumbbells in a single, compact design. This makes them a great option if you're short on space or if you're looking for a cost-effective solution that can grow with you as your strength improves.

Adjustable dumbbells are perfect for progressive overload, a key principle in strength training. You can start with a lighter load and gradually add more weight as your muscles grow stronger. Dumbbells help you challenge your body and push your limits!

Hex Dumbbells: The Stable and Sturdy Option

Last but not least, we have hex dumbbells. The ends of these dumbbells are shaped like hexagons, giving them a unique, six-sided design.

What's the advantage of this shape? Stability. Hex dumbbells won't roll away when you set them down, making them safer for home workouts.

This makes them ideal for exercises that require dumbbells to stay put, like renegade rows or dumbbell push-ups.

Hex dumbbells can be either fixed or adjustable, giving you the best of both worlds. They're sturdy, reliable, and versatile, making them a popular choice among fitness enthusiasts. These are the ones I use, and you'll see them in the movement pictures coming up. I also like them because the weight is rubber and you can drop them when you're tired. No, I'm not saying to throw them (haha!). Because of the rubber ends, you don't have to worry about them rolling away, breaking a toe, or a dumbbell as you drop from a close distance!

These are the three types of dumbbells, each with unique features and benefits. Whether you're a fan of the classic fixed-weight dumbbells, love the versatility of adjustable dumbbells, or prefer the stability of hex dumbbells, there's a dumbbell out there that's just right for you.

Now, with a better understanding of your options, you're well-equipped to navigate the world of dumbbells. You don't need to have the fanciest equipment or the heaviest weights. Find what works best for you and make the most of it!

3.3 Safety Tips for Using Dumbbells

Dumbbells, like any other fitness tool, require a certain level of caution and awareness. Remember, your safety is paramount. Whether you're a seasoned weight lifter or just starting your strength training journey, following a few simple safety tips can go a long way in keeping you injury-free and ensuring your workouts are effective. Let's discuss some of these essential safety tips.

Proper Lifting Technique to Avoid Injury

Correct form is critical to prevent injuries and ensure you're targeting the right muscles.

For each dumbbell exercise, pay careful attention to your posture. Keep your back straight, engage your core, and make sure your movements are controlled and deliberate. Avoid rushing through the exercises. Correctly performing each rep is more important than completing a rep or set as fast as possible.

For example, when doing a dumbbell bicep curl, keep your elbows close to your body and move only your forearms. Avoid jumping to move the weight up or using your back or shoulders to lift the weights. The focus should be on your biceps.

And remember, it's okay to ask for help. If you need help with the correct form, seek advice from a fitness professional or refer to reputable fitness resources.

The Importance of Warming Up Before Lifting Weights

Before diving into your workout, preparing your body with a warm-up is essential. Much like you wouldn't rev up a cold car engine and immediately speed off, you should only jump straight into intense lifting after a good warm-up.

A warm-up increases your heart rate, warms up your muscles, and prepares your body for the workout ahead. It can be as simple as a few minutes of light cardio, like jogging in place or jumping jacks, followed by dynamic stretches that mimic the movements you'll be doing in your workout.

For instance, if you're going to be doing dumbbell lunges, you could warm up with bodyweight lunges, which helps prime your body for the movement and reduces the risk of injury.

How to Choose the Right Weight for Your Fitness Level

Choosing the right dumbbell weight is like picking out shoes - you need the right fit to be beneficial (and avoid discomfort or injury!). The 'right' weight will depend on your fitness level, the specific exercise you're doing, and your training goals.

A general rule of thumb is to choose a weight that challenges you but doesn't compromise your form. If you can't perform the exercise correctly or if you have to use momentum to lift the weight, it's too heavy.

On the flip side, the weight might be too light if you can easily breeze through your reps without feeling any challenge. The last few reps of your set should feel challenging, but you should still be able to maintain proper form.

We've touched on the basics of dumbbell safety! Adopt the right lifting technique, begin with a warm-up, and choose the correct weight. These simple steps can make a significant difference in your strength training routine, helping you avoid injuries and maximize your results. So, let's pick up those dumbbells and get ready to work out - safely and effectively!

3.4 Choosing the Right Dumbbell Weight for You

Selecting the right dumbbell weight for your workout takes time and practice. You have to do the lift to see if it's the right weight but practice it with more repetitions to understand how your body responds to the weight. It shouldn't be too light that it doesn't challenge you, nor too heavy that it compromises your form. It needs to be just right - a weight that stimulates your muscles effectively without causing undue strain. Let's explore how to find your "just right" dumbbell weight.

Starting with a Weight You Can Lift Comfortably for 10-12 Reps

When venturing into the world of strength training, a good starting point is to select a weight you can lift with good form for about 10-12 reps. The final couple of reps should feel challenging but not so challenging that your form breaks down.

Let's say you're doing dumbbell curls. Pick a weight and try to perform 10-12 reps. If you're breezing through the 12th rep, the weight is too light. If you're struggling to complete 8 reps, it's too heavy. But if those last few reps of a 10-12 rep set feel challenging and you can maintain proper form, congratulations! You've found your starting dumbbell weight.

Signs You're Ready to Increase Your Dumbbell Weight

As you progress in your strength training, your muscles will adapt and become stronger. As you become stronger, you must up the ante and increase your dumbbell weight. But how do you know when it's time to level up?

A clear sign is when you can comfortably perform more than 12 reps with perfect form. If you're easily cranking out 15 or 20 reps, it's time to challenge yourself with a heavier dumbbell.

Another sign is if you don't feel fatigued by the end of your set. Remember, those last few reps should feel tough. If they don't, it signals that your muscles are ready for a bigger challenge.

The Importance of Progressing at Your Own Pace

Here's where we need to hit the pause button and talk about something important - your pace. In the race to build strength and muscle, it can be tempting to lift heavier weights sooner. But remember, strength training isn't a sprint; it's a marathon.

Progressing at your own pace means listening to your body and respecting its limits. It means valuing quality over quantity, choosing a weight that allows you to perform each rep with proper form, building a strong foundation, and gradually increasing the intensity of your workouts.

I've been in this strength training game since 2003! There have been times when I pushed my limit on a lift that I wasn't ready for, and it took me out for a week. There have been times when I was doing a lighter lift but felt tired and under the weather that day. I chose not to listen to my body, and guess what? My body responded by telling me I couldn't lift for a week. Again. It's just so important to listen to your body. I have learned my lesson!

I sit here as a 46-year-old woman who loves to lift but has to remind myself daily: don't rush it. Take your time, listen to your body, and increase your weights gradually. Your muscles will thank you, and you'll be less likely to get injured.

Dumbbells are trusted companions in your strength training journey, offering many effective exercises. They promote balanced muscle development, making your workouts efficient and productive. They're also convenient, enabling you to work out at home, in your own space, and at your own pace. I can't wait for you to embrace the full potential of these compact weights and witness the transformative power of strength training!

Chapter 4:
Beginner-Friendly Dumbbell Workouts

Strength training starts with laying a strong foundation and growing into your full potential.

There's something invigorating about your first few workouts. It's a mix of anticipation, determination, and adrenaline. And trust me, that feeling never gets old. Whether it's your first workout or your hundredth, every session allows you to challenge yourself, grow stronger, and feel empowered.

4.1 Strength Work Focus: Full Body Introduction

Here is your introduction to full-body dumbbell movements that target all your major muscle groups. We'll explore four exercises:

1. Dumbbell Squat

2. Dumbbell Deadlift

3. Dumbbell Thruster

4. Dumbbell Bent Over Row

Dumbbell Squat

The Dumbbell Squat is the foundation of strength training. It is versatile, effective, and a staple in any workout routine. It targets your lower body, working your quads, hamstrings, and glutes while engaging your core.

Here's how you do it:

1. Stand with your feet shoulder-width apart, holding a dumbbell in each hand.
2. Lower your body as if sitting back into a chair, keeping your chest up and your knees tracking over your toes.
3. Reach for full depth, meaning hips just below parallel.
4. Push through your heels to stand back up to the starting position.

Think of it like sitting on a low chair and getting back up, keeping those dumbbells close to your body throughout the movement.

Dumbbell Deadlift

Next up, we have the Dumbbell Deadlift, a powerful exercise that works your entire posterior chain - the muscles running up the back of your body, from your heels to your head.

Here's how you do it:

1. Stand with your feet hip-width apart, holding a dumbbell in each hand in front of your thighs.

2. Hinge at your hips, pushing them back as you lower the dumbbells along your shins.

3. Bring the dumbbells to the middle of your shin, all the while pulling the dumbbells towards your shin.

4. Squeeze your glutes and push your hips forward to return to the starting position.

Imagine closing a car door with your hips—that's the movement you want to replicate in a deadlift.

Dumbbell Thrusters

The Dumbbell Thruster combines a front squat and an overhead press. It targets your lower body, upper body, and core all at once, making it a full-body movement.

Here's how you do it:

1. Start with your feet shoulder-width apart, holding a dumbbell in each hand at shoulder level.
2. Push your hips back and down into a squat, keeping your chest up.
3. Explode upward, driving through your heels and using that momentum to press the dumbbells overhead.
4. Finish the movement with your body stacked wrists over shoulders, shoulders over hips, and hips over ankles.
5. Lower the dumbbells back to your shoulders as you descend into your next squat.

Think of it as a rocket launch. Crouch down, build up energy, and then blast off, launching those weights skyward with the power of your whole body.

Dumbbell Bent Over Row

The Dumbbell Bent Over Row is a fantastic move for your upper back and arms.

Here's how you do it:

1. Stand with your feet hip-width apart, holding a dumbbell in each hand.
2. Bend at your hips and knees, lowering your torso until it's almost parallel to the floor.
3. Pull the dumbbells up to your sides, squeezing your shoulder blades together.
4. Lower the dumbbells back down.

Imagine you're starting a lawnmower, pulling those dumbbells up towards your body.

These are the first full-body dumbbell movements we will incorporate into your workouts! Each exercise targets a specific muscle group, giving you a balanced and effective workout.

If you want to try these movements on your own before the guided workouts, remember to warm up and start with light weights first. Take it at your own pace, maintain proper form, and, most importantly, enjoy the process! This is just the beginning of your strength training journey, and every rep brings you one step closer to your goals. So, let's grab those dumbbells and get moving!

For the best results in understanding and perfecting each of the 4 movements above, follow this sequence:

- 12-15 repetitions of each movement
- Do 3-4 sets of each movement (Listen to your body)
- Rest 1 minute after each working set.

4.2 Strength Work Focus: Upper Body

In this section, we'll focus on the upper body, sculpting muscles that look stunning and boost your strength and confidence. Here are the four exercises we will focus on:

1. Dumbbell Bicep Curl
2. Dumbbell Tricep Extension
3. Dumbbell Shoulder Press
4. Dumbbell Chest Press

Dumbbell Bicep Curl

The Dumbbell Bicep Curl targets your biceps - the muscles that flex your elbow and give your arms their toned, sculpted appearance.

Here's how to do it:

1. Stand tall with a dumbbell in each hand, arms fully extended, and palms facing forward.

2. Keeping your elbows tucked in at your sides, slowly curl the weights while contracting your biceps. Keep your upper arms stationary, and continue the movement until your biceps are fully contracted and the dumbbells are at shoulder level.

3. Slowly begin to lower the dumbbells back to the starting position.

Dumbbell Tricep Extension

Next is the Dumbbell Tricep Extension, a fantastic exercise that targets the muscles at the back of your upper arm.

Here's how to do it:

1. Stand with your feet hip-width apart, holding a dumbbell with both hands.

2. Raise the dumbbell over your head until your arms are fully extended.

3. Keeping your upper arms close to your head and elbows in, lower the dumbbell in an arc behind your head until your forearms touch your biceps.

4. Use your triceps to return the dumbbell back to the starting position.

Dumbbell Shoulder Press

The Dumbbell Shoulder Press is an excellent exercise for your shoulders, and it also engages your upper chest and triceps.

Here's how you do it:

1. Stand with your feet shoulder-width apart, holding a dumbbell in each hand.

2. Bring the dumbbells to shoulder level with your palms facing forward.

3. Press the dumbbells upward until your arms are fully extended.

4. Slowly lower the dumbbells back to the starting position.

Dumbbell Chest Press

Lastly, we have the Dumbbell Chest Press, a classic exercise that targets your chest muscles while working your shoulders and triceps.

Here's how you do it:

1. Lie on your back on a bench (or on the floor), holding a dumbbell in each hand at chest level with your palms facing away from you.

2. Press the dumbbells up until your arms are fully extended.

3. Slowly lower the dumbbells back down to the starting position.

These are your four upper-body-focused movements. They target key muscles in your upper body, helping you build strength and definition.

If you want to try these movements on your own before the guided workouts, remember to warm up and start with light weights first. As you perform these moves, remember to focus on the muscle you're working, maintaining a slow, steady pace, and prioritizing form over speed.

For best results in understanding and perfecting each of the 4 movements above, follow this sequence:

- 12-15 repetitions of each movement
- Do 3-4 sets of each movement (Listen to your body)
- Rest 1 minute after each working set.

4.3 Strength Work Focus: Lower Body

Your lower body serves as your foundation, supporting your every move, from walking and climbing stairs to dancing and kicking a soccer ball. In this section, we'll be stepping into four dynamic exercises:

Dumbbell Lunges

1. Dumbbell Goblet Squat
2. Dumbbell Calf Raise
3. Dumbbell Glute Bridge.

Dumbbell Lunges

First is the Dumbbell Lunge, an exercise that targets your quads, hamstrings, and glutes.

Here's how to do it:

1. Stand tall with a dumbbell in each hand, arms fully extended by your sides.
2. Step forward with your right foot, lowering your body until your right knee is bent at a 90-degree angle.
3. Push off your right foot, returning to the starting position.
4. Repeat with your left foot. That's one rep.

Dumbbell Goblet Squat

Next, we have the Dumbbell Goblet Squat. Think of it as a regular squat but with an added twist. It works your quads, hamstrings, and glutes and engages your core and upper body.

Here's how to do it:

1. Stand with your feet shoulder-width apart, holding one end of a dumbbell with both hands at chest level.
2. Lower your body as if sitting back into a chair, keeping your chest up and your knees tracking over your toes.
3. Reach full depth with your hip crease just below your knees.
4. Push through your heels to stand back up to the starting position.

Dumbbell Calf Raise

The Dumbbell Calf Raise is a simple yet effective exercise that targets your calves, the unsung heroes that power your every step, jump, and tip-toe reach.

Here's how to do it:

1. Stand tall with a dumbbell in each hand, arms fully extended by your sides.

2. Raise your heels off the ground, standing on your tiptoes.

3. Slowly lower your heels back down. That's one rep.

Dumbbell Glute Bridge

Last, we have the Dumbbell Glute Bridge, a fantastic exercise that targets your glutes and hamstrings, helping to strengthen your backside.

Here's how to do it:

1. Lie on your back with your knees bent and feet flat on the floor, holding a dumbbell on your hips.

2. Press your heels into the floor, lifting your hips off the ground until your body forms a straight line from your shoulders to your knees.

3. Lower your hips back down.

These are 4 lower-body-focused movements that target key muscles, helping you build strength and definition where it counts.If you want to try these movements on your own before the guided workouts, remember to warm up and start with light weights first.

As you perform these exercises, remember to focus on the muscle you're working, maintain a slow, steady pace, and prioritize form over speed. You're not just going through the motions; you're cultivating strength, enhancing your balance, and boosting your confidence with every rep.

For best results in understanding and perfecting each of the 4 movements above, follow this sequence:

- 12-15 repetitions of each movement
- Do 3-4 sets of each movement (Listen to your body)
- Rest 1 minute after each working set.

4.4 Progress Tracking and Adjustment: Navigating Your Fitness Map

Tracking your progress and making necessary adjustments is key to staying consistent on your fitness journey. It keeps you on track, helps you see how far you've come, and guides you towards your goals. Let's explore how setting realistic goals, recording workouts, monitoring body changes, and adjusting workouts based on progress can keep you moving forward!

Setting Realistic Goals

Having a fitness goal keeps you focused and motivated. They should be realistic, achievable, and aligned with your lifestyle. Perhaps you want to feel stronger, have more energy, or improve your endurance. Maybe you have a specific goal, like being able to do ten push-ups or run a mile without stopping.

Remember, your goals are uniquely yours - they should inspire and motivate you, not stress you out. It's not about achieving perfection or comparing yourself to others but about becoming your best self.

Recording Workouts

Keep a record of your workouts! It tells the story of your fitness journey, capturing triumphs, challenges, and everything in between. Jot down the exercises you do, the weights you lift, and the number of reps and sets you complete. Note how you feel during and after each workout - energized, tired, strong, or sore. (I have already made a workout logbook for you! Check it out!) https://a.co/d/4i5hxo6

This fitness diary serves as a tangible record of your efforts and progress. It can motivate you on tough days, remind you of your strengths, and help you see patterns or trends, like when you feel most energetic or which exercises you enjoy the most.

Monitoring Body Changes

Your body is a reflection of your lifestyle, including your workouts and eating habits. Pay attention to how it changes over time. You might notice increased muscle tone, improved posture, or enhanced flexibility. Maybe your clothes fit differently, or you have more energy throughout the day! Write these things down in your logbook!

Remember, these changes extend beyond physical appearances. Strength training can boost mood, improve sleep, and enhance overall well-being. Celebrate these victories—they're proof of your hard work and dedication.

Adjusting Workouts Based on Progress

Your progress guides your fitness journey. It tells you when to adjust your workouts—to add more weights, try new exercises, or challenge your endurance.

As you get stronger, your current workout routine may become less challenging. That's your cue to level up - increase the dumbbell weight, add more reps or sets, or introduce new exercises into your routine.

On the flip side, if you're feeling consistently tired or noticing a decline in progress, it might be a sign you're overdoing it and need to scale back. Remember, rest and recovery are vital parts of the equation.

Navigating your fitness journey is a dynamic process. It involves setting realistic goals, tracking your workouts, observing changes in your body, and adjusting your workouts as needed. Tune into your body, respect its signals, and move in a direction that brings you closer to your goals.

I have changed my fitness goals so many times in the last 20-25 years! I've gone through 3 pregnancies, trained for many endurance events, trained for sprint events, and trained for weightlifting competitions! My fitness goals change based on each event! When I was training for a 10k or half marathon, I consistently strength trained, but my focus turned toward building stamina and endurance for those runs. In CrossFit competitions, my focus shifted towards specific movement strength, where I needed to deadlift a very heavy weight for my team! So, strength and stamina were my focus because we still had to move heavy weights quickly in those competitions.

More recently, my goals have shifted to progressive overload, balance training, and keeping my body strong, flexible, and ready for fun! As a 46-year-old woman, my body is changing, and keeping muscle on my body is my number one priority. However, I still love to surf, hike, and play pickleball with my family, so I train for fun too!

Through it all, I have had fitness trackers, workout logbooks, and strength apps to track all my runs, strength workouts, and fitness workouts! Looking at where I started and shaping my goals moving forward is fun and keeps me motivated. I hope the same for you!

Chapter 5:
Intermediate Dumbbell Workouts

It's important to push and challenge yourself in Strength Training constantly. This next section offers some new and slightly more difficult movements to challenge your muscles, fire up your metabolism, and learn to push past your comfort zone.

These are the 4 movements we are focusing on for this section:

1. Dumbbell Single Leg Deadlift

2. Dumbbell Renegade Row

3. Dumbbell Bulgarian Split Squat

4. Dumbbell Push Press

5.1 Strength Work Focus: Full Body Challenge

Dumbbell Single Leg Deadlift

The Dumbbell Single Leg Deadlift is similar to the Dumbbell Deadlift we did in Chapter 4. But this time, you are balancing on one leg. This powerful exercise works your entire posterior chain - the muscles running up the back of your body, from your heels to your head. However, by standing on one leg, you are also focusing on balance.

Here's how you do it:

1. Stand with your feet hip-width apart, holding a dumbbell in one hand next to your thigh. (You can also do this by holding a dumbbell in each hand.)

2. Hinge at your hips, pushing them back as you raise the leg of the opposite weight behind you. Lower the dumbbell while keeping it close to your leg to activate your back, shoulder, and core.

3. Bring the dumbbell to the middle of your shin, all the while pulling the dumbbells towards your shin.

4. Squeeze your glutes and push your hips forward to return to the starting position.

Dumbbell Renegade Row

The Dumbbell Renegade Row is a challenging exercise that combines a plank, a pushup, and a row. It works your core, back, and arms while testing your stability and endurance.Here's how to do it:

1. Get into a high plank position, holding a dumbbell in each hand.

2. Bring your chest to the ground to do a pushup (chest touching the ground, elbows back).

3. As you come out of the pushup, row one dumbbell up to your side, squeezing your shoulder blade.

4. Bring the dumbbell back to the ground and lower your whole body to a pushup position (chest touching the ground.)

5. Lower the dumbbell and repeat with the other arm.

One way to remember the movement is to tell yourself:

- Pushhup
- Right row
- Pushup
- Left row

That makes one rep.

Make sure to keep your body stable with each pull. Keep the core and glutes tight.

Dumbbell Bulgarian Split Squat

The Dumbbell Bulgarian Split Squat targets your quads, hamstrings, and glutes while challenging your balance and coordination.

Here's how you do it:

1. Stand a couple of feet from a bench, holding a dumbbell in each hand.
2. Place the top of one foot on the bench behind you.
3. Bend your front knee, lowering your body until your front thigh is parallel to the floor.
4. Push through your front heel to rise to the starting position.

Dumbbell Push Press

The Dumbbell Push Press is a dynamic exercise that combines a shoulder press with a bit of momentum from your lower body. It targets your shoulders, arms, and core.

Here's how to do it:

1. Stand with your feet hip-width apart, holding a dumbbell in each hand at shoulder level.

2. Bend your knees slightly, then push up explosively, using that momentum to press the dumbbells overhead.

3. Lower the dumbbells back to your shoulders.

These intermediate workouts are designed to challenge you, push your boundaries, and help you discover new strengths!

If you want to do them before the guided workouts in chapter 10, make sure to warm up and use light weights first. For best results in understanding and perfecting each of the 4 movements above, follow this sequence:

- 12-15 repetitions of each movement

- Do 3-4 sets of each movement (Listen to your body)

- Rest 1 minute after each working set.

5.2 Strength Work Focus: Targeting the Core

Your core is the epicenter of your body, a powerhouse that supports every movement, from lifting and bending to balancing and twisting. It's your body's command center, coordinating your muscles to move in harmony. In this section, we are going to focus on this crucial area with four targeted exercises:

1. Dumbbell Russian Twist

2. Dumbbell Plank Row

3. Dumbbell Windmill

4. Dumbbell Side Bend

Dumbbell Russian Twist

The Dumbbell Russian Twist is a dynamic exercise that targets your obliques, the muscles on the sides of your stomach. It's a fun, challenging move that also engages your entire core.

Here's how you do it:

1. Sit on the floor with your knees bent, holding a dumbbell with both hands in front of your chest.

2. Lean back slightly, keeping your back straight.

3. Twist your torso to the right, bringing the dumbbell towards your right hip.

4. Repeat on the left side. That's one rep.

Visualize yourself as a pendulum, swinging from side to side. Keep your movements smooth and controlled, letting your core do the work.

Dumbbell Plank Row

Next up, we have the Dumbbell Plank Row. This exercise combines a plank and a row, working your core, back, and arms.

Here's how you do it:

1. Get into a high plank position, holding a dumbbell in each hand.
2. Keeping your body stable, row one dumbbell up to your side, squeezing your shoulder blade.
3. Lower the dumbbell and repeat with the other arm.

Dumbbell Windmill

The Dumbbell Windmill is a unique exercise that targets your obliques and challenges your shoulder stability.

Here's how you do it:

1. Stand with your feet wider than shoulder-width apart, holding a dumbbell in your right hand.

2. Extend your right arm overhead, and turn your feet slightly to the left.

3. Slide your left hand down your left leg, extending your right arm.

4. Push your hips to the right, bending at the waist until your torso is nearly parallel to the floor.

5. Reverse the movement to return to the starting position.

Dumbbell Side Bend

Last, we have the Dumbbell Side Bend, an exercise that targets your obliques and helps improve your side-to-side stability.

Here's how you do it:

1. Stand tall with a dumbbell in your left hand, palm facing inwards.

2. Bend at your waist to the left sliding the dumbbell down your side.

3. Return to the start position and repeat, then repeat on the right side.

These core-focused exercises help you build strength and stability in your midsection. Remember to maintain a steady pace and prioritize form over speed as you engage in these exercises. Stay focused, breathe deeply, and focus on your core!

If you want to do these movements before the guided workouts, make sure to warm up first and start with light weights to get the movement right! For best results in understanding and perfecting each of the 4 movements above, follow this sequence:

- 12-15 repetitions of each movement

- Do 3-4 sets of each movement (Listen to your body)

- Rest 1 minute after each working set.

5.3 Strength Work Focus: Strength and Endurance

In fitness, strength, and endurance go hand in hand, each complementing the other. These next four exercises are designed to boost both your strength and endurance. They are:

1. Dumbbell Farmer's Walk

2. Dumbbell Step Up

3. Dumbbell Swing

4. Dumbbell Push Up

Dumbbell Farmer's Walk

First up, we have the Dumbbell Farmer's Walk, an exercise that's as straightforward as it sounds. It's all about carrying heavy weights (in our case, dumbbells) and walking, just like a farmer would do in the fields.

Here's how you do it:

1. Stand tall, a dumbbell in each hand, arms by your side.

2. Engage your core, roll your shoulders back, and start walking.

3. Take slow, measured steps, maintaining an upright posture.

4. You can walk for 30 seconds in one direction, then 30 seconds back. Or you can use a measured distance.

Dumbbell Step Up

The Dumbbell Step-Up works your quads, hamstrings, and glutes while also challenging your balance.

Here's how you do it:

1. Stand in front of a step or bench, a dumbbell in each hand.
2. Place your right foot on the step, and push through your heel to lift your body up till your left foot reaches the top of the box or bench.
3. Stand up straight.
4. Lower back down and repeat with the left foot.

Dumbbell Swing

The Dumbbell Swing is a dynamic move that targets your hips, glutes, hamstrings, and core. It's like a pendulum, the dumbbell swinging back and forth, powered by your hips.

Here's how you do it:

1. Stand with your feet hip-width apart, holding one end of a dumbbell with both hands.

2. Hinge at your hips, letting the dumbbell swing back between your legs.

3. Thrust your hips forward, propelling the dumbbell up to shoulder height.

4. Let the dumbbell swing back down, and repeat.

Dumbbell Push Up

Lastly, we have the Dumbbell Push Up, a challenging variation of the classic push-up that works your chest, shoulders, triceps, and core.

Here's how you do it:

1. Get into a high plank position, holding a dumbbell in each hand.
2. Lower your body, bending your elbows back until your chest is just above the floor.
3. Push back up to the starting position.

These exercises are designed to challenge you, pushing your strength and endurance to new limits. As you perform these moves, remember to focus on your form and control, using your breath to power through each rep. You're not just going through the motions; you're nurturing your strength, boosting your stamina, and pushing past boundaries you never thought possible.

For best results in understanding and perfecting each of the 4 movements above, follow this sequence and remember to use lighter weights so you can get the form right!:

- 12-15 repetitions of each movement
- Do 3-4 sets of each movement (Listen to your body)
- Rest 1 minute after each working set.

5.4 Assessing Your Progress

Tracking Strength Gains

I'm curious how you are feeling at this point in the book. Have you tried the movements so far? If you have, way to go! Doing these movements and learning them as we go will help you when we get to the guided workouts at the end!

Remember to record your weights, reps, and sets. This record serves as a tangible testament to your progress, a diary detailing your strength gains. It highlights your growing abilities, fueling your motivation and building momentum.

Noticing Endurance Improvements

Let's shift our gaze to another crucial facet of your fitness transformation - endurance. This is your body's ability to withstand physical effort for prolonged periods. It's your breath carrying you through an intense workout, your muscles pushing past fatigue, and your heart steadily pumping fuel to your hardworking cells.

Are you finding it easier to get through your workouts? Can you maintain a high level of effort for longer? These are signs of improved endurance, a testament to your body's growing efficiency and resilience.

Observing Body Composition Changes

Take a moment to appreciate your hard work. Have you noticed changes in how your clothes fit? Do you see more muscle definition and a more sculpted appearance? These visible changes are signs of improved body composition, a shift toward more muscle and less fat.

Body composition changes are like footprints on the sand, marking your progress on this fitness adventure. They're visual cues of your transformation, reminders of your dedication and hard work.

Remember, these changes extend beyond the mirror. They're reflected in how you feel - stronger, more energetic, more confident. It's the embodiment of your strength training efforts, your body wearing the badges of your progress with pride.

Chapter 6:
Advanced Dumbbell Workouts

This chapter is about embracing a new challenge with dumbbells! We are going to dive into the world of advanced dumbbell workouts.

Over the past few chapters, we've built a solid foundation with the dumbbell movements we have learned, and now it's time to try some advanced workouts that will challenge us, inspire us, and help us discover even more of our potential. The four new movements we will learn are:

1.   Dumbbell Snatch

2.   Dumbbell Clean and Press

3.   Dumbbell Turkish Get-Up

4.   Dumbbell Man Maker

6.1 Strength Work Focus: Full Body Blast

Dumbbell Snatch

The Dumbbell Snatch is a full-body exercise requiring power, precision, and focus.

Here's how to do it:

1. Stand with your feet shoulder-width apart, a dumbbell between your feet.

2. Bend at your hips and knees, grab the dumbbell, and in one swift movement, pull it upwards.

3. As the dumbbell ascends, extend your body, hopping slightly off the ground, and pull yourself under the dumbbell.

4. Catch the dumbbell overhead with your arm fully extended, then stand up straight.

Dumbbell Clean and Press

The Dumbbell Clean and Press is a two-part movement involving a clean and an overhead press.

Here's how you do it:

1. Stand with your feet hip-width apart, a dumbbell in each hand.

2. Bend your knees and hips to lower the dumbbells along your shins

3. In one explosive movement, pull the dumbbells up to your shoulders (the clean) and then press them overhead.

4. Lower the dumbbells back to your shoulders, then to the starting position.

Dumbbell Turkish Get Up

The Dumbbell Turkish Get Up is a slow, deliberate sequence of movements that takes you from lying down to standing up.

Here's how you do it:

1. Lie on your back, holding a dumbbell in your right hand, arm fully extended.

2. Bend your right knee and place your right foot flat on the floor.

3. Prop yourself up on your left elbow, then push up onto your left hand.

4. Lift your hips off the ground, then sweep your left leg back to kneel.

5. Push through your right foot to stand up, keeping the dumbbell overhead.

6. Reverse the steps to return to the starting position.

Dumbbell Man Maker

The Dumbbell Man Maker is a series of movements requiring high focus, coordination, and strength.

Here's how you do it:

1. Start in a high plank position, holding a dumbbell in each hand.

2. Perform a push-up, then row one dumbbell up to your side, followed by the other.

3. Jump your feet in, then stand up and press the dumbbells overhead.

4. Lower the dumbbells back to the floor and jump your feet back to return to the starting position.

For best results in understanding and perfecting each of the 4 movements above, follow this sequence:

- 5-10 repetitions of each movement
- Do 3-4 sets of each movement (Listen to your body)
- Rest 1 minute after each working set.

These are the Full-Body Blast workout movements that will challenge every muscle. These exercises are advanced, so take it slow, keep your form in check, and always listen to your body. It's an excellent time to focus on your goals. Learning these movements will challenge your body and your mind. Anytime we do that, we are making considerable strides in our lives and taking us closer to our personal goals!

6.2 Strength Work Focus:
High-Intensity Interval Training (HIIT)

HIIT is a type of interval training that requires you to work in short bouts to get the heart rate up, followed by a rest period. HIIT workouts are all about increased intensity. In this section, we will use our Dumbbells to get our heart rate up quickly, which builds heart strength and stamina. The four movements we will focus on are:

1. Dumbbell Burpees

2. Dumbbell Mountain Climbers

3. Dumbbell Skiier Swing

4. Dumbbell Jump Squat

Dumbbell Burpees

Dumbbell Burpees fare a dynamic, full-body exercise that gets your heart racing and muscles working.

Here's how you do it:

1. Stand tall, clutching a dumbbell in each hand by your sides.

2. Bring the dumbbells down to the ground like you would in a deadlift. (hinge at the hips, bend your knees and keep your back flat).

3. Kick (or step) your feet behind into a high plank, maintaining a firm grip on the dumbbells, and let your chest touch the ground.

4. Push up through your arm and spring your feet forward, returning to the deadlift position.

5. Rise to standing.

Think of it as a rapid dance sequence, transitioning from one move to the next with fluidity and control.

Dumbbell Mountain Climbers

Dumbbell Mountain Climbers is a high-intensity exercise that fires up your core, arms, and legs.

Here's how you do it:

1. Start in a high plank position, each hand gripping a dumbbell.

2. Drive your right knee toward your chest, bring your right foot up to your right hand, then quickly extend it back to the plank position.

3. Repeat the movement with your left knee and foot. That's one rep.

Dumbbell Skier Swing

The Dumbbell Skier Swing targets your hips, glutes, hamstrings, and core.

Here's how you do it:

1. Stand with your feet hip-width apart, a dumbbell in each hand by your sides.

2. Hinge at your hips, allowing the dumbbells to swing back between your legs.

3. Explosively extend your hips, propelling the dumbbells forward up to chest height.

Visualize the graceful arc of a pair of skis, your body mirroring this rhythm as you swing the dumbbells with power and precision.

Dumbbell Jump Squat

The Dumbbell Jump Squat is a powerful exercise that engages your lower body, core, and heart rate.

Here's how you do it:

1. Stand with your feet shoulder-width apart, holding a dumbbell in each hand at your sides.
2. Lower into a squat, keeping your chest upright.
3. Explosively push through your heels, jumping off the ground and extending your legs.
4. Land softly, transitioning directly into your next squat.

With these high-intensity interval training (HIIT) workouts, you're building strength and endurance, enhancing your cardiovascular health, boosting your metabolism, and challenging your body in new and exciting ways. So, I hope you try these new movements and get ready to sweat, push, and conquer!

Remember, if you want to do these movements before the guided workout, follow this sequence:

- 5-10 repetitions of each movement
- Do 3-4 sets of each movement (Listen to your body)
- Rest 1 minute after each working set.

6.3 Strength Work Focus: Supersets for Strength

Supersets are two exercises performed back-to-back with little to no rest in between. They're a time-efficient way to increase the intensity of your workouts, stimulate muscle growth, and elevate your heart rate. With supersets, you're strengthening your muscles, challenging your endurance, and boosting your metabolism.

Here are the three powerful supersets we will be doing:

1. Dumbbell Bench Press and Dumbbell Row
2. Dumbbell Squat and Dumbbell Deadlift
3. Dumbbell Bicep Curl and Dumbbell Tricep Extension

Dumbbell Bench Press and Dumbbell Row

Our first superset pairs the Dumbbell Bench Press, an exercise for your chest, shoulders, and triceps, with the Dumbbell Row, an exercise for your upper back and arms.

Here's how you do it:

1. Start with the Dumbbell Bench Press. Lie on your back on a bench (or on the floor), holding a dumbbell in each hand at chest level. Press the dumbbells up until your arms are fully extended. Lower the dumbbells back down to the starting position.

2. Without resting, switch to the Dumbbell Row. Stand with your feet hip-width apart, holding a dumbbell in each hand. Hinge at your hips, letting your arms hang down, palms facing in. Pull the dumbbells up to your sides, squeezing your shoulder blades. Lower the dumbbells back down.

Perform 8-12 reps of these two exercises back-to-back, then take a 1-2 minute rest before repeating the superset.

Dumbbell Squat and Dumbbell Deadlift

Next is the Dumbbell Squat and Dumbbell Deadlift superset, a lower body powerhouse that targets your quads, hamstrings, and glutes.

Here's how you do it:

1. Start with the Dumbbell Squat. Stand with your feet shoulder-width apart, holding a dumbbell in each hand. Lower your body as if sitting back into a chair, keeping your chest up and your knees tracking over your toes. Push through your heels to stand back up to the starting position.

2. Without resting, switch to the Dumbbell Deadlift. Stand with your feet hip-width apart, holding a dumbbell in each hand in front of your thighs. Hinge at your hips, pushing them back, as you lower the dumbbells along your shins. Squeeze your glutes and push your hips forward to return to the starting position.

Perform 8-12 reps of these two exercises back-to-back, then take a 1-2 minute rest before repeating the superset.

Dumbbell Bicep Curl and Dumbbell Tricep Extension

Our final superset are excellent exercises for your arms - the Dumbbell Bicep Curl and the Dumbbell Tricep Extension.

Here's how you do it:

1. Start with the Dumbbell Bicep Curl. Stand tall with a dumbbell in each hand, arms fully extended, and palms facing forward. Keeping your elbows tucked in at your sides, slowly curl the weights while contracting your biceps. Continue the movement until your biceps are fully contracted, and the dumbbells are at shoulder level. Lower the dumbbells back to the starting position.

2. Without resting, switch to the Dumbbell Tricep Extension. Stand with your feet hip-width apart, holding a dumbbell with both hands. Raise the dumbbell over your head until your arms are fully extended. Keeping your upper arms close to your head and elbows in, lower the dumbbell in an arc behind your head until your forearms touch your biceps. Use your triceps to return the dumbbell back to the starting position.

Perform 8-12 reps of these two exercises back-to-back, then take a 1-2 minute rest before repeating the superset.

6.4 Celebrating Your Achievements

Recognizing Strength Improvements

Think about the first time you picked up a dumbbell. Can you remember the weight? How about the number of reps or sets you did? Now, think about the present moment. How much weight are you lifting now? Have you increased the number of reps or sets? The ability to lift heavier weights, or perform more reps or sets, is a clear indicator of improved strength. It's a tangible measure of progress, a sign that your muscles are growing stronger and more capable.

Take a moment to appreciate this progress. It's a testament to your hard work, dedication, and resilience. It's proof that you can push your limits, overcome challenges, and achieve your goals.

Appreciating Endurance Enhancements

Let's turn the spotlight to another vital aspect of your fitness transformation - endurance. Remember how you felt after your first few workouts? Did you feel out of breath, with your heart pounding and muscles needing a break? Now, compare that with how you feel after your current workouts. Can you push through intense sessions without feeling like you're about to pass out? Can you recover faster between sets? These are signs of improved endurance.

Endurance is your body's ability to withstand physical effort over time. It's about how long you can keep going before fatigue sets in. It's a measure of your heart and lung efficiency, your muscle resilience, and your mental grit. Improved endurance means you're getting fitter, healthier, and tougher! I hope you are able to stop and appreciate your progress!

Acknowledging Body Transformation

Now, let's talk about the changes you can see and feel - your body transformation. Have you noticed your clothes fitting differently? Are your muscles more defined? Do you feel stronger, more energetic, more confident? These changes are signs of improved body composition, a shift toward more muscle and less fat.

Body transformation is more than just about losing weight or looking good. It's about building a strong, healthy body that serves you well. It's about feeling good in your own skin, radiating confidence, and embracing your unique beauty. So, take a good look in the mirror. Appreciate the body you've trained, the strength you've cultivated, and the person you've become. You're not just transforming your body; you're transforming your life.

Celebrating Consistency and Dedication

Last, let's celebrate your consistency and dedication. Showing up for your workouts, day after day, week after week, requires commitment. It's about making a promise to yourself and keeping it. It's about putting in the work, even when you're not in the mood or progress seems slow.

Consistency is the golden thread that weaves through every successful fitness story. It's the habit that turns an ambitious goal into an achievable reality. I hope you've shown up for yourself, put in the work, and stayed committed to your fitness journey. That's a victory worth celebrating!

Chapter 7:
Nutrition for Muscle Growth and Recovery

Welcome to Chapter 7, where we'll explore the world of macros and micros, the essential nutrients that fuel our bodies. We'll dive into proteins, carbohydrates, fats, vitamins, and minerals, understanding their roles and significance in muscle growth and overall health.

7.1 Understanding Macros and Micros

Proteins: Building Blocks of Muscles

Think of proteins as the bricks of your body's construction site. Just like bricks form the foundation of a building, proteins are fundamental to the structure of your cells. They're involved in nearly all cell functions, from repairing tissues to constructing enzymes, hormones, and immune molecules.

But when it comes to strength training, proteins shine as the building blocks of muscles. When you perform a strength training workout, you create microscopic tears in your muscles. Proteins come to the rescue, repairing these tears and, in the process, making your muscles stronger.

So, how do you incorporate proteins into your diet? Here are a few protein-rich foods to consider:

- Lean meats like chicken and turkey
- Fish such as salmon and tuna
- Dairy products like milk, cheese, and yogurt
- Plant-based proteins including lentils, chickpeas, and quinoa

Carbohydrates: Energy Providers

Carbohydrates are the fuel for your body's engine. They provide the energy your body needs to function, from powering your brain to fueling your workouts.

When you consume carbohydrates, your body breaks them down into glucose, which is used for immediate energy, or stored in your muscles and liver as glycogen for later use. During a workout, your body taps into these glycogen stores for energy, keeping you going through those squats and lunges.

Here are some carbohydrate-rich foods to include in your diet:

- Whole grains like oatmeal, brown rice, and whole wheat bread
- Fruits such as bananas, apples, and berries
- Vegetables like sweet potatoes, peas, and corn
- Legumes such as lentils, chickpeas, and black beans

Fats: Essential for Hormonal Balance

Fats often get a bad rap, but they're actually essential for your body's function. They provide a concentrated source of energy, help absorb vitamins, and are crucial for hormonal balance.

In the context of strength training, fats play a supportive role. They provide the energy needed for longer workouts and help maintain healthy testosterone levels, which is important for muscle growth.

Here are some sources of healthy fats:

- Avocados
- Nuts and seeds
- Fatty fish like salmon and mackerel
- Olive oil

Vitamins and Minerals: For Overall Health

Finally, we have vitamins and minerals, the unsung heroes of your body's function. They're involved in many processes, from supporting immune function to aiding in energy production.

While they don't directly contribute to muscle growth, vitamins and minerals support your overall health, ensuring your body can perform at its best. For instance, calcium and vitamin D are essential for bone health, while B vitamins help your body convert nutrients into energy.

Here are some ways to get a variety of vitamins and minerals in your diet:

- Eat a rainbow of fruits and vegetables, each color representing different nutrients.
- Include a variety of lean proteins, whole grains, and healthy fats.
- Consider a multivitamin supplement if you cannot meet your nutrient needs through diet alone.

Understanding macros and micros is like having a roadmap for a balanced diet. It guides your food choices, ensuring you fuel your body with the nutrients it needs to function at its best. So, apply this knowledge to your diet, and remember, every meal is an opportunity to nourish your body.

7.2 Pre- and Post-Workout Nutrition: Fueling Your Fitness

Protein-Rich Snacks Before Workouts

Your workout begins long before you pick up those dumbbells. It starts with fueling your body and providing it with the energy it needs to power through the exercises. Think of protein as your pre-workout ally, supplying your muscles with the amino acids they need to perform and recover.

A protein-rich snack about an hour before your workout can set the stage for a productive session. It provides a steady stream of amino acids, helping to prevent muscle breakdown during the workout. Something as simple as a hard-boiled egg, a piece of chicken, or a protein shake can do the trick.

Remember, this is not about loading up on protein. It's about giving your body a small dose of this crucial nutrient to optimize your performance and recovery. So, before your next workout, consider adding some protein to your pre-workout routine and notice the difference it makes.

Carbohydrate and Protein Balance After Workouts

Once you've wrapped up your workout, it's time to shift gears to recovery mode. This is where carbohydrates and protein come into play. Together, they kick-start the recovery process, helping to replenish your energy stores and repair your muscles.

Carbohydrates are your body's go-to source of energy. Consuming carbohydrates after a workout helps replenish the glycogen stores that you've depleted during your training session. It's like refueling your car after a long drive.

Conversely, protein provides the building blocks your muscles need to repair the microscopic tears caused by strength training.

A post-workout meal or snack that includes both carbohydrates and protein can enhance your recovery and support muscle growth. Consider a turkey or tuna sandwich on whole-grain bread, a bowl of quinoa with roasted veggies and chicken, or a simple protein shake with a banana.

Importance of Post-Workout Hydration

Hydration is the unsung hero of your workout performance and recovery. It's involved in numerous bodily functions, including transporting nutrients, eliminating waste, and maintaining optimal body temperature.

During a workout, your body loses water and electrolytes through sweat. Rehydrating after exercise is crucial to replacing these losses, supporting recovery, and preparing your body for the next workout.

The amount of fluid you need depends on the intensity of your workout and how much you sweat. A good rule of thumb is to drink at least half a liter of water for every half an hour of intense exercise. You might need more if you've had a particularly sweaty session.

Remember, hydration isn't just about water. Electrolytes, especially sodium and potassium, are also important as they help to maintain fluid balance in your body. A post-workout snack or meal with a balance of fluids and electrolytes can help you rehydrate more effectively. So, don't forget to replenish your fluids after your workout. Your body will thank you.

In the grand scheme of your fitness endeavor, nutrition is paramount. It's the fuel that powers your workouts, the building blocks that support your recovery, and the hydration that keeps everything running smoothly. Planning your pre- and post-workout nutrition requires a strategy and some prep time.

For example, my mornings are full of 4-6 hours straight of training my amazing clients. I get so hungry, and I have to get my workout done when I'm done training my clients. If I have an early morning of training, I plan and prep my morning snack the night before and have it in the refrigerator waiting for me. It's full of protein, carbs, fiber, and fat and keeps me sustained for coaching clients and my workout coming up. If I didn't plan, I'd eat the first thing I saw in front of me because I get so hungry. It probably would not be healthy; then I wouldn't have the energy to work out when I'm done with my clients! So taking that extra ten minutes the night before is everything I need to keep me moving forward!

7.3 Hydration and Muscle Health

Water's Role in Muscle Function

Let's look deeper into muscle health and the role hydration plays. Imagine each muscle cell is like a miniature water tank. These tanks need to be filled to the brim for optimal function. Water, being a major component of our cells, is crucial for muscle contractions and relaxation.

When you curl those dumbbells or perform a squat, your muscle fibers slide past each other, creating tension and movement. Water facilitates this process by acting as a lubricant, reducing friction and enabling smooth, coordinated muscle contractions.

Additionally, water also plays a key role in nutrient transport. It's like your body's delivery system, shuttling nutrients like glucose for energy and amino acids for muscle repair to your muscle cells. Without ample hydration, this delivery process can be slowed down, impacting your muscle function and recovery.

Signs of Dehydration

Now, let's talk about the flip side - dehydration. Picture a lush, vibrant plant wilting under the scorching sun, its leaves drooping and losing their vitality. That's what happens to our muscles when we're dehydrated. It's not a pretty sight!

Common signs of dehydration include fatigue, dizziness, and headaches. But what does it mean for your muscles? When you're dehydrated, your muscle cells can't hold onto as much water, impairing their function. This can lead to muscle fatigue, decreased strength, and prolonged recovery time.

One specific sign of dehydration during a workout is muscle cramps. These painful, involuntary muscle contractions are often a result of fluid and electrolyte imbalance in your muscle cells. If you've ever experienced a sudden, sharp pain in your calf or foot during a workout, you've likely had a taste of what muscle cramps feel like.

Tips for Staying Hydrated

Staying well-hydrated is super important! Here are some practical tips for keeping your hydration levels in check:

1. Make Water Your Go-To Beverage: It's calorie-free, readily available, and does a fantastic job at hydrating your body. Keep a water bottle handy, especially during workouts.

2. Hydrate Before, During, and After Workouts: Sip on water before you start exercising, take small gulps every 15-20 minutes during your workout, and rehydrate once you're done. If you're doing a long, intense workout, consider a sports drink to replenish lost electrolytes.

3. Eat Water-Rich Foods: Foods like cucumbers, watermelon, and oranges are not only tasty but also packed with water. Including them in your diet can help boost your hydration status.

4. Listen to Your Body: Thirst is your body's way of signaling that it's time to drink up. However, don't wait until you're parched. Sip on water throughout the day to keep your hydration levels topped up.

In the grand scheme of strength training, hydration plays a huge role. It's your body's lifeline, essential for muscle function, nutrient transport, and overall performance, and it keeps your body running like a well-oiled machine!

7.4 Meal Planning and Prep Tips: Stepping into the Kitchen Lab

Your kitchen is a place where you can experiment with ingredients, discover new flavors, and create meals that nourish your body and satisfy your taste buds. How do you decide what to cook, how much to eat, and when to shop? This section is all about guiding you through this process, offering practical tips on meal planning, preparation, portion control, and grocery shopping.

Weekly Meal Planning

Weekly Meal planning is the most important task in planning your meals for the week, ensuring each one aligns with your nutritional needs and fitness goals.

Start by setting aside some time each week to plan your meals. This could be a quiet Sunday afternoon or a relaxed weekday evening. Consider your schedule for the week - will you be home for dinner every night, or do you have social events planned? Do you need to pack lunches for work or school?

Once you have an idea of the number of meals you'll need, start planning the dishes. Aim for a balance of proteins, carbohydrates, and fats in each meal, and don't forget to include plenty of fruits and vegetables. A grilled chicken salad with a side of whole grain bread, a stir-fry with lean beef and veggies, or a hearty lentil soup are all great options.

Remember, meal planning is not about creating elaborate menus or cooking gourmet meals. It's about organizing your meals in a way that supports your fitness journey while also satisfying your taste buds.

For a family of 5 like myself, I choose 5 proteins for the week and 5 complimentary carbs and veggie dishes that go with it! This keeps it very simple for me! I make larger amounts so I can have leftovers and lunches for the next few days. I also stock up on veggies and spend the time cutting them and putting them in containers so I can easily access them. Otherwise, they go into my fridge to rot.

Simple and Nutritious Recipe Ideas

Now that you have a meal plan, it's time to figure out what to cook. Here's where you can let your creative juices flow, experimenting with different recipes and flavors.

Keep a collection of simple and nutritious recipes at your fingertips. These can be from cookbooks, websites, or even handed down from your family. My countertop has cookbooks and binders filled with recipes I have printed from different websites over the years! The key is to find recipes that are easy to prepare, packed with nutrients, and delicious.

Our family has a few staples. One is a simple stir-fry with your choice of protein (usually chicken or ground turkey), a rainbow of veggies, and a flavorful sauce put over rice. Another dinner we love, especially in the summer, is a big salad with grilled chicken, lots of crunchy veggies, and a yummy dressing. We also love chili with lean ground turkey, veggies, and beans. We put it over baked sweet potatoes or rice.

Remember, variety is the spice of life. Don't be afraid to try new recipes or experiment with different flavors. Cooking should be a joy, not a chore.

Portion Control Tips

Portioning out your food in the right amount helps you determine how much to eat. Learning about and understanding serving sizes is important, as is listening to your hunger and fullness cues and eating mindfully.

A simple way to visualize portion sizes is by using your hand as a guide. A serving of protein should be about the size of your palm, a serving of carbohydrates the size of your fist, and a serving of fats the size of your thumb.

When serving your meals, try using smaller plates or bowls. This can trick your mind into thinking you're eating more than you actually are. Also, try to eat without distractions like TV or your phone. This can help you eat more mindfully and recognize when you're full.

Remember, portion control doesn't mean deprivation. It's about enjoying a variety of foods in amounts that support your fitness goals and overall health.

Efficient Grocery Shopping

Grocery shopping can feel like navigating a maze, with tempting treats at every turn. But with a little planning and a few smart strategies, you can easily navigate the supermarket. Make a grocery list based on your meal plan. It can help you stay focused and prevent impulse buys. Try to shop the perimeter of the store first, where fresh foods like fruits, vegetables, dairy, and meats are. Save the inner aisles, where more processed foods are found, for last.

When buying packaged foods, pay attention to the nutrition labels. Look for foods that are low in added sugars and high in fiber and protein.

Remember, the supermarket is your gateway to a myriad of nutritious foods. Approach it with a plan, navigate it confidently, and you'll come out with a cart full of wholesome ingredients ready to fuel your body and workouts.

So, I'd like to be really honest with you about grocery shopping and cooking. Stepping into the kitchen and cooking healthy food was never easy or fun for me. If I'm really honest, it has stressed me out more than I want to let on. I think grocery shopping for a family of five is hard. I try to do it once a week and plan it all out before I go! So it's a big trip, and I am focused the whole time on buying a lot of food for the week. Over the years, spending more time in the kitchen cooking meals, asking for help, and having the kids chip in with ideas for meals has made it a lot easier and gratifying! We also work together to unload the groceries and they help me meal plan and clean up. It makes it so much better!

I have had to learn to take time to think and meal prep before even thinking about walking into a grocery store! Looking at recipes and planning what I need for each meal has helped reduce the stress. I also found that using an app on my phone to help me with my grocery list and bringing a little friend (one of my cutie kids) always perks up my spirits!

Figuring out which recipe I want to use and then following it has helped me grow in my confidence in cooking. When everyone loves a new dish I made, I feel even better, knowing it was a healthy homemade meal! Now, I can make meals up on my own and only refer to recipes now and then! It has been a road for me. But I want you to know: If I can do it, so can you!

I hope you can experience the joy of cooking, the satisfaction of nourishing your body, and the pleasure of savoring your creations!

Chapter 8:
Healthy Habits
for a Lifetime of Strength

In this chapter, we'll explore the power of consistency in training, the importance of giving equal attention to different types of workouts, and the art of adapting workouts to fit your schedule. We'll also dive into the importance of sleep for muscle recovery, stress management techniques to complement your exercise routine, and the significance of incorporating active rest days into your training schedule.

8.1 Importance of Consistency in Training

When it comes to strength training, showing up is half the battle. I have been training myself and clients for over 20 years. What I've learned is that it doesn't matter how you show up, you just need to show up. When I was coaching classes at my CrossFit gym, I told new members that all they had to do was walk through the doors to my class, because it is half the battle! I would take care of the rest! That is my hope with this book and this chapter in particular that you would learn that you don't always have to want or desire to workout; you just need to start.

Regular Training for Muscle Growth

Your muscles respond to the demands you put on them. When you engage in regular strength training, you send them a clear message: "We need to build more muscle to meet these demands."

Here's how you can make regular training part of your routine:

- Schedule your workouts: Treat your workouts like important appointments. Write them in your calendar, set reminders, and make sure to show up.

- Make it manageable: You don't need to spend hours at the gym to see results. Short, intense workouts can be just as effective. Aim for 30 minutes of strength training three to four times a week.

- Mix it up: Variety keeps things interesting. Switch up your exercises, try different types of strength training (like bodyweight exercises or resistance band workouts), and challenge yourself with new routines.

Balancing Different Types of Workouts

Just like a balanced diet provides a variety of nutrients, a balanced workout routine offers a range of benefits.

Consider these tips to create a balanced routine:

- Combine strength and cardio: While strength training builds muscle, cardiovascular exercise like running or cycling improves heart health and burns calories. Both are important for overall fitness.

- Work all major muscle groups: Make sure your routine includes exercises for all the major muscle groups: legs, hips, back, abdomen, chest, shoulders, and arms.

- Include flexibility and balance exercises: Activities like yoga or pilates can improve your flexibility and balance, complementing your strength training routine and reducing the risk of injuries.

Adapting Workouts to Your Schedule

Finding time for workouts can be a challenge. But with a little creativity, you can fit exercise into even the busiest schedule.

Here are some strategies:

- Break it up: If you can't set aside a 30-minute block for exercise, try doing short bursts of activity throughout the day. Ten minutes in the morning, ten minutes at lunch, and ten minutes in the evening can add up to a full workout.

- Make it a habit: Try linking your workouts to a regular part of your routine, like doing a quick workout while your coffee brews in the morning, or doing a workout while watching TV in the evening.

- Use what you have: If you can't get to the gym, use what you have at home. Bodyweight exercises or workouts with simple equipment like dumbbells or resistance bands can be just as effective.

Incorporating these strategies into your fitness routine can help you stay consistent with your workouts, bringing you closer to your strength training goals. Remember, consistency is key, balance is beneficial, and adaptability is advantageous. With these principles in mind, you can cultivate a successful strength training routine that fits your lifestyle and supports your fitness journey.

8.2 The Role of Sleep in Muscle Recovery

Sleep and Muscle Repair

During strength training workouts, your muscles undergo microscopic damage, which is a normal part of the muscle-building process. However, it's during sleep that these tiny tears are repaired, and new muscle tissue is formed. This is thanks to the growth hormone, which is released during the deep stages of sleep and aids in muscle repair and growth.

So, while you're dreaming sweet dreams, your body is hard at work, building strength and resilience.

Tips for Quality Sleep

So, how can you ensure you get quality sleep to support muscle recovery? Here are a few tips to craft your slumber strategy:

- Regular Sleep Schedule: Aim to go to bed and wake up at the same time every day, even on weekends. This can help regulate your body's internal clock and improve the quality of your sleep.

- Sleep-Friendly Environment: Create a restful environment that's dark, quiet, and comfortably cool. Consider using earplugs, an eye mask, or a white noise machine if needed.

- Screen-Free Time: Try to turn off electronic devices at least an hour before bed. The light emitted by screens can interfere with your body's production of melatonin, a hormone that regulates sleep.

- Relaxation Techniques: Activities such as reading, taking a warm bath, or practicing gentle yoga can help signal your body that it's time to wind down and go to sleep.

Remember, good sleep habits don't happen overnight. It takes consistency and patience, but the rewards are well worth the effort.

Impact of Sleep Deprivation on Performance

Now, let's consider the flip side of the coin - what happens when you skimp on sleep? Picture a smartphone with a low battery, sluggish, slow to respond, and unable to perform at its best. That's what your body can feel like when you're sleep-deprived.

Lack of sleep can affect performance in many ways. It can slow reaction times, impair concentration, and sap motivation. It can also compromise the immune system, making you more susceptible to illnesses and injuries.

Sleep deprivation can interfere with muscle recovery and growth during strength training. It can also affect your body's ability to store glycogen, a form of energy used during workouts, which impacts stamina and performance.

In essence, sleep deprivation is like trying to drive a car with a flat tire. It can slow you down, hinder your progress, and make your fitness journey a whole lot bumpier. So, make sleep a priority, and you'll be cruising down the path to strength and fitness with a fully charged battery and all cylinders firing.

8.3 Stress Management and Exercise

Exercise as a Stress Reliever

Physical activity triggers the release of endorphins, your body's natural mood lifters. These 'feel-good' hormones act as natural painkillers, helping to reduce stress and induce feelings of relaxation and positivity. Whether it's a vigorous dumbbell workout or a brisk walk around the block, exercise can be a potent stress reliever.

So, the next time you feel tense or overwhelmed, consider reaching for your dumbbells or lacing up your walking shoes. Use exercise as your secret weapon against stress, a haven where you can leave your worries behind and emerge feeling calm and rejuvenated.

Mindfulness Techniques for Stress Reduction

Imagine you're a tightrope walker, balancing on a thin wire high above the ground. Your entire focus is on maintaining your equilibrium, each step deliberate and measured. This level of attention, this deep sense of awareness, is the essence of mindfulness.

Incorporating mindfulness techniques into your exercise routine can enhance the stress-relieving benefits of physical activity. It's about immersing yourself in the present moment, tuning into your body's movements, and reconnecting with your breath.

One simple technique is to focus on your breath as you exercise. Notice the rhythmic flow of air, the rise and fall of your chest, and the sensation of your breath entering and leaving your body. This can help clear your mind, reduce stress, and enhance your focus.

Another technique is to tune into your body's movements. Pay attention to the feeling of your muscles contracting and relaxing, the sensation of your feet hitting the ground, or the weight of the dumbbells in your hands. This can help you stay present, improve your performance, and infuse a sense of calm into your workouts.

Remember, mindfulness is not about achieving a particular state or feeling. It's about noticing what's happening in the present moment without judgment. It's about creating a space of calm amid the chaos, a tranquil oasis where stress dissipates and peace prevails.

Balancing Exercise and Relaxation

While exercise is a powerful stress reliever, relaxation techniques can further enhance your body's ability to combat stress. Techniques such as deep breathing, meditation, and yoga can help lower your heart rate, reduce blood pressure, and promote a sense of calm and well-being.

Consider setting aside some time each day for relaxation. It could be a few minutes of deep breathing in the morning, a short meditation session after your workout, or some gentle yoga stretches before bed. This can help to balance the intensity of your workouts with the tranquility of relaxation, creating a symphony of fitness that nurtures not just your body but also your mind.

Remember, exercise and relaxation are two sides of the same coin, each one enhancing the other.

8.4 Incorporating Active Rest Days

Importance of Rest Days

Rest days are an integral part of an effective strength training program. They allow your muscles to repair, rebuild, and strengthen. They also give your nervous system a chance to recuperate. While it might seem counterintuitive, taking time off from your workouts can enhance your progress. During these rest periods, your body adapts to the stress of exercise, and the real training effect takes place.

Active Rest Day Activities

Now, let's explore the concept of active rest days. I think of them as an opportunity to keep your body moving without taxing your muscles. Think of active rest days as a gentle nudge to your body, a way to promote circulation, enhance mobility, and boost your mood while giving your muscles a well-deserved break.

Active rest activities are lower in intensity and provide a contrast to your regular strength training routine. These could include light cardiovascular exercises such as walking, cycling, or swimming. They could also involve flexibility and balance exercises such as yoga or pilates. The aim is to move your body in a way that feels restorative, not exhaustive.

Listening to Your Body

Are you feeling more tired than usual? Are your muscles sore for more than a couple of days? Is your performance declining? These could be signs that your body needs a break. Remember, it's okay to take a rest day. It's okay to slow down. In fact, it's more than okay - it's necessary.

Chapter 9:
Overcoming Common Challenges: Making Dumbbell Workouts Work for You

In this chapter, we will address how you can best carve out time for strength training and how you can fit your dumbbell workouts into your busy schedule! Let's explore!

9.1 Fitting Workouts into Your Busy Schedule

Short and Effective Workouts

Your workouts can be short and effective! Strength training, particularly with dumbbells, allows for intense workouts that can be done in a short span of time. By focusing on compound exercises like squats, lunges, and deadlifts, you can engage multiple muscle groups at once, maximizing your workout efficiency.

For instance, a 20-minute workout could look like this:

- Dumbbell Squats: 10 reps

- Dumbbell Deadlifts: 10 reps

- Dumbbell Lunges: 10 reps for each leg

- Dumbbell Overhead Press: 10 reps

- Dumbbell Rows: 10 reps each arm

Repeat this circuit three times with a minute of rest between each circuit. In just 20 minutes, you've worked your entire body and stoked your metabolism!

Making the Most of Your Time

Think of your daily schedule as a jigsaw puzzle, each piece representing a task or commitment. Fitting in a workout is like finding the perfect spot for that tricky piece - it might require some maneuvering, but there's always a way!

Can you wake up 30 minutes earlier for a quick dumbbell workout? Can you utilize your lunch break for an efficient circuit? How about turning your TV time into a training session? Even on the busiest days, look for pockets of time that can be used for a quick workout.

Integrating Exercise into Daily Activities

Integrating exercise into your daily activities can make your workouts more manageable and less time-consuming.

Consider these suggestions:

- Use a dumbbell as a paperweight and perform a set of bicep curls between emails.

- Store a pair of dumbbells near your sofa and do a set of overhead presses during commercial breaks.
- While waiting for your morning coffee to brew, use those precious minutes to complete a quick dumbbell circuit.

Incorporating dumbbell exercises into mundane tasks not only saves time but also adds an element of fun to your daily routine. Find the opportunity to move, strengthen, and grow any chance you get!

Remember, your fitness regimen isn't a one-size-fits-all. It is designed to fit the unique contours of your life. It's about finding what works for you, adapting your workouts to your schedule, and embracing the flexibility that dumbbell training offers.

9.2 Dealing with Plateaus

Recognizing a Plateau

Plateau's in strength training happen. It might feel like you're putting in the work, but your progress seems to stall.

Signs of a plateau can include a lack of improvement in your strength or endurance, an inability to increase the weight you're lifting, or a decrease in motivation. You might also notice that your workouts feel less challenging or that your body composition isn't changing despite your consistent efforts.

Recognizing a plateau is the first step toward overcoming it. It's about being aware of your progress, tuning into your body, and acknowledging when something isn't working. It's about understanding that a plateau isn't a dead end, but a part of the process, a sign that it's time to shake things up.

Strategies to Overcome Plateaus

Now that you've recognized a plateau, it's time to tackle it head-on. Think of it as a puzzle, a challenge that requires a fresh perspective and a strategic approach.

1. Mix Up Your Routine: If you've been doing the same exercises for a while, your body may have adapted to them, reducing their effectiveness. Try incorporating new exercises into your routine, changing the order of your workouts, or varying the number of sets and reps you perform.

2. Increase Intensity: Consider upping the intensity of your workouts. This could mean lifting heavier weights, shortening rest periods, or incorporating advanced techniques like supersets or drop sets.

3. Prioritize Recovery: Overtraining can also lead to plateaus. Make sure you're taking enough rest days, getting quality sleep, and eating a balanced diet to support your muscle recovery and growth.

4. Set New Goals: Setting new fitness goals can reignite your motivation and help you push past a plateau. This could be aiming to lift a certain weight, mastering a new exercise, or working towards a specific body composition goal.

Remember, overcoming a plateau is like finding a detour on a blocked road. It might require a bit of trial and error, but with persistence and creativity, you can find a way around it and continue on your path to strength and fitness.

Importance of Patience and Persistence

In the grand scheme of fitness, patience and persistence are the main focus. They're the dynamic duo that turns setbacks into comebacks, obstacles into opportunities, and plateaus into launching pads for growth.

Patience is about understanding that progress takes time. It's about trusting the process, knowing that every workout, every rep, and every lift is bringing you closer to your goals, even if you can't see the results right away.

Persistence, on the other hand, is about showing up, even when progress slows down. It's about sticking with your workouts, staying committed to your goals, and believing in your ability to overcome challenges.

In the face of a plateau, patience and persistence can be relied on. They remind you that progress is not always linear, that ups and downs are part of the journey, and that every step, no matter how small, is a step in the right direction.

So, as we navigate the ups and downs of our strength training adventure, let's hold onto patience and persistence. Try to embrace the plateaus as opportunities for growth, reminders of our resilience, and stepping stones on our path to strength and fitness. After all, the view from the top is worth every twist and turn it takes to get there. So, let's keep going, one step, one rep, one lift at a time.

9.3 Preventing and Treating Common Injuries

Proper Form and Technique

Paying careful attention to the form and technique of your dumbbell exercises is paramount. Proper form is the cornerstone of safe and effective strength training. It ensures that you're targeting the right muscles, minimizing the risk of injury, and getting the most out of every rep.

Consider the Dumbbell Deadlift, a classic exercise that targets your hamstrings, glutes, and lower back. Begin with the dumbbells at your feet, palms facing your body. Bend at the hips and knees, maintaining a straight back. Grab the dumbbells and press through your heels to rise to a standing position, keeping the dumbbells close to your body. Reverse the movement to lower the dumbbells back to the floor.

Incorrect form, such as rounding your back or letting the dumbbells drift away from your body, can strain your back and lead to injury. By focusing on proper form, you can perform the Dumbbell Deadlift safely, effectively, and confidently.

Importance of Warm Up and Cool Down

A warm-up gently prepares your body for the workout ahead. It increases your heart rate, warms up your muscles, and enhances your joint mobility. A simple warm-up could involve 5-10 minutes of light cardio, such as brisk walking or jogging, followed by some dynamic stretches.

Just as a warm-up prepares your body for a workout, a cool-down helps your body transition back to a state of rest. It allows your heart rate and breathing to return to normal, helps remove waste products from your muscles, and reduces the risk of post-exercise dizziness. Your cool-down could involve 5-10 minutes of light cardio, such as slow walking, followed by static stretches.

By incorporating a warm-up and cool-down into your routine, you're treating your body with the care it deserves, reducing the risk of injuries, and enhancing your overall workout experience.

Recognizing and Responding to Pain

Consider the beep of a smoke detector, alerting you to potential danger. In many ways, pain serves a similar purpose in your body. It's an alarm bell, alerting you to potential harm. Learning to recognize and respond to this alarm is paramount to safe strength training.

While a certain degree of muscle soreness is normal after a workout, sharp or persistent pain is a red flag. For instance, if you experience a sharp pain in your shoulder during a Dumbbell Overhead Press, it's crucial to stop the exercise immediately to avoid further injury.

If you experience pain during a workout, follow the RICE method - rest, ice, compression, and elevation. Rest the affected area, apply ice to reduce swelling, use a bandage to compress the area, and elevate the area to reduce inflammation.

If the pain persists, seek medical attention. A healthcare professional can provide an accurate diagnosis and appropriate treatment plan to help you safely return to your workouts.

Strength training, like any physical activity, carries a risk of injury. But by prioritizing proper form, warming up and cooling down, and listening to your body's signals, you can significantly reduce this risk. After all, your goal is to build strength and health, not to sideline yourself with an injury. So, take it slow, pay attention to your body, and remember - safety first!

9.4 Staying Motivated and Committed

Setting Realistic Goals

Let's talk about setting realistic goals that are tangible and achievable.

First, take a moment to reflect on what you hope to achieve with your dumbbell workouts. Are you looking to build strength, lose weight, or simply establish a regular exercise habit? Once you've identified your overarching goal, break it down into smaller, measurable objectives. For instance, if your goal is to build strength, a smaller objective might be to increase the weight you're lifting by a certain amount over a specific period.

By setting realistic goals, you're not only giving your workouts a clear purpose but also creating a sense of accountability that can help keep you motivated.

Celebrating Progress

In the whirlwind of reps, sets, and workouts, it's easy to lose sight of the progress you're making. That's why it's important to take a step back from time to time and celebrate how far you've come. Have you increased the weight you're lifting? Are your clothes fitting better? Do you feel stronger and more energetic? These are all signs of progress, and they deserve to be recognized and celebrated.

We've talked about this before, but I will keep returning to it because it is so important. Consider keeping a workout journal where you can track your workouts (remember I have already made one for you!), note any increases in weight or reps, and record how you're feeling. Not only will this provide a tangible record of your progress, but it can also serve as a powerful motivator when your motivation is running low.

Finding a Workout Buddy

Having a workout buddy can make the process more enjoyable, increase your motivation, and even boost your performance. I have had a few workout buddies over the years. Right now, I strength train alone, but every week, I meet up with a friend for a walk. My favorite thing about this friend is that she likes to walk fast! It makes me laugh because we both check our pace on our fitness watches to see if we are keeping up with our pace from the previous week! One of the last times we went for our usual walk, neither of us had to be anywhere afterward, so we kept walking, talking, laughing, and keeping pace. When I came home and checked my walk distance on my fitness app, we unknowingly walked 6 miles! And we had the best time doing it!

Your workout buddy could be a friend, a family member, or a colleague who shares similar fitness goals. Together, you can cheer each other on, share tips and advice, and hold each other accountable. On days when your motivation is flagging, knowing that someone else is counting on you can be just the push you need to stick with your workout plan.

Remember, strength training isn't meant to be a solitary journey. It's a path that can be shared, enjoyed, and celebrated with others. So, find a workout buddy, lace up your shoes, and embark on this fitness adventure together. After all, the road to strength is always more enjoyable when traveling with a friend.

You've got the tools, the guidance, and the motivation. Now it's time for action. So, pick up those dumbbells, embrace the challenge, and remember: every rep, every lift, every drop of sweat is a step closer to a stronger, healthier, more empowered you. Let's get lifting!

Chapter 10:
BONUS CHAPTER,
21-Day Workout Challenge!

Workout Methodology Explained

Are you excited for your 21-Day Workout? I am! I created these workouts with evidence-based research on me and my clients! The workouts provided are programmed as a 3-day split:

- Day 1 of each week is Lower Body

- Day 2 of each week is Upper Body

- Day 3 of each week is Full Body

You can do one, two, or three of the workouts every week. I wanted to make it doable for you at whatever stage you are!

21 workouts at 3 days a week gives you a 7-week workout. Make a note of each workout you complete in your workout logbook. After week 7, start week 8 with Day 1/Week 1; raise those weights from what you recorded in your journal, or add more reps to each set!

My goal is to give you a 30-minute workout. You will need to do a warmup and cooldown stretches on your own.

Warm Up:

- Start each workout with a 2-minute walk, row, or stationary bike.
- Warm up your shoulder and hip joints with leg swings and arm swings (be gentle!).
- Add dynamic stretches, especially those that align with your workout. Full-body stretches will suffice.
- I will always give you a 3-round warm-up before we move into the workout.

Cool down: Walk for 2 minutes. Finish with some static holds and deep breathing.

As a reminder, each of the exercises below has pictures and movement descriptions in the above chapters. You will have to go back and review the movements to make sure you are doing them correctly. This is no different than when I train my in-person clients. We always review the movement description and movement pattern with light weights before we move into the workout and add challenging weights.

LET'S DO THIS!!!

7 weeks: Lower Body, Upper Body, Full Body

Week 1:

Day 1: Lower Body

Warm Up: Complete 3 rounds at your own pace:

- 10 Dumbbell Swings

- 10 Body weight Air Squats
- 10 Dumbbell pushups

Strength 1: Complete 5 rounds of this superset; resting one minute after the step-ups:

- 6 Dumbbell Deadlifts
- 10 left leg/10 right leg Dumbbell Step-ups

Strength 2: Complete 4 rounds of this superset; resting one minute after the plank:

- 8L/8R Dumbbell Bulgarian Split Squat
- 45-second plank from your elbows

Finisher: Complete 4 rounds, resting one minute after the Russian Twists:

- 10 Dumbbell Glute Bridge
- 10 Dumbbell Russian Twists

Day 2: Upper Body

Warm Up: Complete 3 rounds at your own pace:

- 10 Dumbbell pushups
- 10L/10R Dumbbell side bends
- 30-Second Farmer Carry

Strength 1: Complete 5 rounds of this Superset (rest one minute after the Tricep Extensions)

- 10 Dumbbell Chest press (from the ground or a bench)
- 10 Dumbbell Tricep Extensions

Strength 2: Complete 5 rounds of this Superset (rest one minute after the bicep curls)

- 10 Left/10 Right Bent over Dumbbell Row
- 10 Dumbbell Bicep Curls

Finisher: Complete 3 rounds as fast as possible of:

- 5 Dumbbell Renegade Row
- 20 Dumbell Mountain Climber

Day 3: Full Body

Warm Up: Complete 3 rounds at your own pace:

- 10 Dumbbell Swings
- 45 Second Dumbbell Plank
- 10 Left/10 Right Light Dumbbell Step-ups

Strength 1: Complete 5 rounds of this Superset, resting one minute after Push Press

- 10 Dumbell Squat
- 10 Dumbell Push Press

Strength 2: Complete 4 rounds of this Superset, resting one minute after the situps

- 10 Left/10 Right Dumbbell Lunges
- 15 Situps

Finisher: Complete 3 rounds as fast as possible of:

- 10 DB burpees
- 10 bodyweight jump squats

Week 2:

Day 1: Lower Body

Warm Up: Complete 3 rounds at your own pace:

- 10 Dumbbell Swings
- 10 Body weight Air Squats
- 10 Dumbbell pushups

Strength 1: Complete 5 rounds of this superset; resting one minute after the step-ups:

- 10 Dumbbell Squats
- 10 left leg/10 right leg Dumbbell Step-ups

Strength 2: Complete 4 rounds of this superset; resting one minute after the calf raises:

- 8L/8R Dumbbell Bulgarian Split Squat
- 10 Dumbbell Calf Raises

Finisher: Complete 4 rounds, resting one minute after the Goblet Squats:

- 10 Dumbbell Glute Bridge
- 10 Dumbbell Goblet Squats

Day 2: Upper Body

Warm Up: Complete 3 rounds at your own pace:

- 10 Dumbbell pushups
- 10L/10R Dumbbell side bends
- 30-Second Farmer Carry

Strength 1: Complete 5 rounds of this Superset (rest one minute after the Bicep Curls)

- 10 Dumbbell Push Press
- 10 Dumbbell Bicep Curl

Strength 2: Complete 5 rounds of this Superset (rest one minute after the bicep curls)

- 10 Tricep Extensions
- 10 Sitting Dumbbell Bicep Curls

Finisher: Complete 3 rounds as fast as possible of:

- 10 Dumbbell Clean and Press
- 20 Dumbell Russian Twist

Day 3: Full Body

Warm Up: Complete 3 rounds at your own pace:

- 10 Dumbbell Swings
- 45 Second Dumbbell Plank
- 10 Air Squats

Strength 1: Complete 5 rounds of this Superset, resting one minute after Plank

- 10 Dumbell Thrusters
- 1-minute Dumbell Plank

Strength 2: Complete 4 rounds of this Superset, resting one minute after the situps

- 10 Left/10 Right Dumbbell Single Leg Deadlift
- 15 Situps

Finisher: Complete 3 rounds as fast as possible of:

- 10 Dumbbell Chest Press
- 10 Dumbbell Glute Bridge

Week 3:

Day 1: Lower Body

Warm Up: Complete 3 rounds at your own pace:

- 15 Dumbbell Swings
- 15 Body weight Air Squats
- 20 Situps

Strength 1: Complete 5 rounds of this superset; resting one minute after the calf raises:

- 8 Dumbbell Deadlift (increase weight from last time)
- 15 Dumbbell Calf Raises

Strength 2: Complete 4 rounds of this superset; resting one minute after the step-ups:

- 8L/8R Dumbbell Bulgarian Split Squat
- 10L/10R Dumbbell Step Ups

Finisher: Complete 4 rounds, resting one minute after the Single Leg Deadlift:

- 15 Dumbbell Glute Bridge
- 10/10 Single Leg Deadlift

Day 2: Upper Body

Warm Up: Complete 3 rounds at your own pace:

- 10 Air Squats
- 10L/10R Dumbbell side bends
- 10 Light Dumbell Shoulder Press

Strength 1: Complete 5 rounds of this Superset (rest one minute after the Tricep Extensions)

- 10 Dumbbell Chest Press
- 10 Dumbbell Tricep Extensions

Strength 2: Complete 5 rounds of this Superset (rest one minute after the Renegade Rows)

- 10 left/10 right Dumbbell Bent over Row
- 10 Dumbbell Renegade Row

Finisher: Complete 3 rounds as fast as possible of:

- 10 Left/10 Right Dumbbell Snatch
- 20 Dumbell Russian Twist

Day 3: Full Body

Warm Up: Complete 3 rounds at your own pace:

- 10 Dumbbell Deadlift (lightweight)
- 45 Second Dumbbell Plank
- 10 Air Squats

Strength 1: Complete 5 rounds of this Superset, resting one minute after Plank

- 10 Left/10 Right Dumbbell Single Leg Deadlift
- 1-minute Dumbell Plank

Strength 2: Complete 4 rounds of this Superset, resting one minute after Tricep Extensions

- 10Left/10Right Dumbbell Step Ups
- 10 Standing Dumbbell Bicep Curls
- 10 Dumbbell Tricep Extensions

Finisher: Complete 3 rounds as fast as possible of:

- 5 Dumbbell Man Makers
- 10 Dumbbell Jumping Squats

Week 4:

Day 1: Lower Body

Warm Up: Complete 3 rounds at your own pace:

- 10 Left/10 Right Body Weight Step Ups
- 15 Body weight Air Squats
- 10 Dumbbell Pushups

Strength 1: Complete 5 rounds, resting one minute after the squats:

- 10 Dumbbell Squat (increase weight from last time)
- 5 Dumbbell Goblet Squat

Strength 2: Complete 4 rounds of this superset; resting one minute after the step-ups:

- 8L/8R Dumbbell Bulgarian Split Squat
- 10L/10R Dumbbell Step Ups

Finisher: Complete 4 rounds, resting one minute after the Plank:

- 15 Dumbbell Glute Bridge
- 1 minute Plank

Day 2: Upper Body

Warm Up: Complete 3 rounds at your own pace:

- 10 Air Squats
- 10L/10R Dumbbell side bends
- 10 Light Dumbell Chest Press

Strength 1: Complete 5 rounds of this Superset (rest one minute after the Mountain Climbers)

- 10 Dumbbell Push Press
- 20 Dumbbell Mountain Climbers

Strength 2: Complete 5 rounds of this Superset (rest one minute after the tricep extensions)

- 15 Dumbbell Bicep Curl
- 15 Dumbbell Tricep Extensions

Finisher: Complete 3 rounds as fast as possible of:

- 5 Dumbbell Turkish Get-Ups
- 1 minute Farmer Carry Walk

Day 3: Full Body

Warm Up: Complete 3 rounds at your own pace:

- 20 Steps Body Weight only Walking Lunges
- 10 Dumbbell Pushups
- 10 Dumbbell Swings

Strength 1: Complete 5 rounds of this Superset, resting one minute after Russian Twists

- 10 Left/10 Right Bulgarian Split Squat
- 20 Dumbbell Russian Twists

Strength 2: Complete 4 rounds of this Superset, resting one minute after Bent Over Row

- 10Left/10Right Dumbbell Step Ups
- 10 Dumbbell Chest Press
- 10 Dumbbell Bent Over Row

Finisher: Complete 3 rounds as fast as possible of:

- 10 Dumbbell Burpees
- 20 Situps

Week 5:

Day 1: Lower Body

Warm Up: Complete 3 rounds at your own pace:

- 10 Dumbbell Swings
- 15 Body weight Air Squats

- 10 Dumbbell Pushups
- 10 Dumbell Deadlift (Light)

Strength 1: Complete 5 rounds, resting one minute after the deadlift:

- 10 Dumbbell Deadlift (increase weight from last time)

Strength 2: Complete 4 rounds of this superset; resting one minute after the step-ups:

- 8L/8R Dumbbell Single Leg Deadlift
- 10L/10R Dumbbell Step-Ups

Finisher: Complete 3 rounds as fast as possible:

- 15 Dumbbell Glute Bridge
- 10L/10R Body Weight Bulgarian Split Squat with a jump

Day 2: Upper Body

Warm Up: Complete 3 rounds at your own pace:

- 10 Air Squats
- 10 Dumbbell Swings
- 10L/10R Dumbbell side bends
- 10 Light Dumbell Shoulder Press

Strength 1: Complete 5 rounds of this Superset (rest one minute after the Situps)

- 10 Dumbbell Chest Press
- 20 Situps

Strength 2: Complete 5 rounds of this Superset (rest one minute after the Tricep Extensions)

- 15 Dumbbell Bicep Curl
- 15 Dumbbell Tricep Extensions

Finisher: Complete 3 rounds as fast as possible of:

- 10L/10R Dumbbell Snatch
- 1 minute Farmer Carry Walk

Day 3: Full Body

Warm Up: Complete 3 rounds at your own pace:

- 10/10 Body Weight only Step Ups
- 10 Dumbbell Pushups
- 10 Dumbbell Swings
- 10 Body Weight Air Squats

Strength 1: Complete 5 rounds of this Superset, resting one minute after Plank Row

- 10Left/10Right Dumbbell Lunges
- 20 Dumbbell Plank Row

Strength 2: Complete 4 rounds of this Superset, resting one minute after Bent Over Row

- 10Left/10Right Dumbbell Bulgarian Split Squat
- 10 Dumbbell Chest Press
- 10 Dumbbell Bent Over Row

Finisher: Complete 3 rounds as fast as possible of:

- 20 Dumbbell Mountain Climbers
- 10 Dumbbell Jumping Squats

Week 6:

Day 1: Lower Body

Warm Up: Complete 3 rounds at your own pace:

- 10 Dumbbell Swings
- 15 Body weight Air Squats
- 10 Dumbbell Pushups
- 1 minute Dumbbell Plank

Strength 1: Complete 5 rounds, resting one minute after the Squats:

- 10 Dumbbell Goblet Squats (increase weight from last time)

Strength 2: Complete 4 rounds of this superset; resting one minute after the step-ups:

- 8L/8R Dumbbell Lunges
- 10L/10R Dumbbell Step-Ups

Finisher: Complete 3 rounds as fast as possible:

- 20 Dumbbell Glute Bridge
- 5L/5R Dumbbell Bulgarian Split Squat

Day 2: Upper Body

Warm Up: Complete 3 rounds at your own pace:

- 10 Air Squats

- 10 Dumbbell Swings
- 10L/10R Dumbbell side bends
- 10 Light Dumbell Bent Over Row

Strength 1: Complete 5 rounds of this Superset (rest one minute after the Row)

- 10 Dumbbell Chest Press
- 10 Dumbbell Single Arm Bent Over Row

Strength 2: Complete 5 rounds of this Superset (rest one minute after Tricep Extensions)

- 15 Dumbbell Bicep Curl
- 15 Dumbbell Tricep Extensions

Finisher: Complete 3 rounds as fast as possible of:

- 15 Dumbbell Clean and Press
- 1 minute Dumbbell Plank

Day 3: Full Body

Warm Up: Complete 3 rounds at your own pace:

- 10/10 Body Weight only Step Ups
- 10 Dumbbell Pushups
- 10 Dumbbell Swings
- 10 Body Weight Air Squats

Strength 1: Complete 5 rounds of this Superset, resting one minute after Plank Row

- 15 Dumbbell Thrusters
- 20 Dumbbell Plank Row

Strength 2: Complete 4 rounds of this Superset, resting one minute after Bent Over Row

- 10Left/10Right Dumbbell Bulgarian Split Squat
- 10 Dumbbell Chest Press
- 10 Dumbbell Bent Over Row

Finisher: Complete 3 rounds as fast as possible of:

- 10L/10R Dumbbell Step Ups
- 10 Dumbbell Jumping Squats
- 10 Dumbbell Pushups

Week 7:

Day 1: Lower Body

Warm Up: Complete 3 rounds at your own pace:

- 10 Dumbbell Swings
- 15 Body weight Air Squats
- 10 Dumbbell Pushups
- 10L/10R Dumbbell Side Bends

Strength 1: Complete 5 rounds, resting one minute after the Deadlifts:

- 12 Dumbbell Deadlift (increase weight from last time)

Strength 2: Complete 4 rounds of this superset; resting one minute after the Step-Ups:

- 8L/8R Dumbbell Single Leg Deadlifts
- 10L/10R Dumbbell Step-Ups

Finisher: Complete 3 rounds as fast as possible:

- 10 Dumbbell Burpees
- 5L/5R Dumbbell Bulgarian Split Squat

Day 2: Upper Body

Warm Up: Complete 3 rounds at your own pace:

- 10 Air Squats
- 10 Dumbbell Swings
- 1 Minute Dumbbell Farmer Carry

Strength 1: Complete 5 rounds of this Superset (rest one minute after the Russian Twists)

- 10 Dumbbell Push Press
- 20 Dumbbell Russian Twists

Strength 2: Complete 5 rounds of this Superset (rest one minute after Tricep Extensions)

- 10 Dumbbell Renegade Row
- 15 Dumbbell Bicep Curl
- 15 Dumbbell Tricep Extensions

Finisher: Complete 3 rounds as fast as possible of:

- 5L/5R Dumbbell Turkish Get Up
- 10 Dumbbell Swings

Day 3: Full Body

Warm Up: Complete 3 rounds at your own pace:

- 10/10 Body Weight only Step Ups
- 10 Dumbbell Pushups
- 10 Dumbbell Swings
- 10 Body Weight Air Squats

Strength 1: Complete 5 rounds of this Superset, resting one minute after Calf Raises

- 10/10 Dumbbell Single Leg Deadlift
- 20 Dumbbell Calf Raises

Strength 2: Complete 4 rounds of this Superset, resting one minute after Bent Over Row

- 10Left/10Right Dumbbell Bulgarian Split Squat
- 10 Dumbbell Chest Press
- 10 Dumbbell Bent Over Row

Finisher: Complete 3 rounds as fast as possible of:

- 10L/10R Dumbbell Step Ups
- 10 Thrusters

Conclusion

I want to thank you for stepping into my gym with me for this book! If you didn't know, the pictures of all the movements are of me, taken by my husband, in my garage gym that I train my clients out of! I wanted to let you know that so you can feel connected to me and know that I do these workouts. I am committed to encouraging women to do these workouts and be the best version of themselves!

The day I did the pictures, I put on the same workout clothes I wear at home, threw my hair up in a ponytail, didn't do any fancy makeup, and had my husband use my iPhone with zero edits.

I am a woman over 40, using strength training to age gracefully.

I am committed to aging gracefully and naturally, and I feel a bit insecure having myself on the cover and all over the book.

But this is me. Natural and imperfect me.

I hope you join me in this movement of finding balance in strength training, cardio, healthy eating, and rest. Nothing comes quick and easy, but it is worth it in the long run.

Your Fitness Journey: A Recap

We've journeyed through the essence of strength training, the miracle of muscle growth, the power of dumbbells, and the importance of nutrition. We've navigated the challenges of fitting workouts into a busy schedule, pushing past plateaus, and preventing injuries. Along the way, we've celebrated the small victories, the personal triumphs, and the incredible progress you've made.

Maintaining Momentum

Remember, this journey doesn't end the moment you put this book down. Think of it as a snowball rolling down a hill, gathering momentum as it goes. Your job is to keep that snowball rolling and keep the momentum going. Your strength training journey doesn't stop here - it continues every time you pick up a dumbbell, every time you push past your comfort zone, and every time you choose to prioritize your health.

The Power of Perseverance

In this pursuit of strength and health, perseverance is your most powerful ally. It's the fuel that keeps your engine running, the spark that keeps your fire burning. There will be days when motivation wanes, when progress stalls and when the weights feel heavier than usual. On those days, remember why you started. Remember the goals you've set, the progress you've made, and the strength you've discovered. Then, dust off those dumbbells and keep going.

Keep Learning, Keep Growing

Remember, knowledge is a journey, not a destination. There's always more to learn, more to explore, more to discover. Keep asking questions, keep seeking answers, keep expanding your understanding of your body and its capabilities. The more you learn, the more you'll grow - not just in strength, but in confidence, resilience, and self-belief.

Next Steps: Your Call to Action

So, what's your next step? Maybe it's adding a new exercise to your routine, increasing your weights, or focusing on your nutrition. Maybe it's setting a new fitness goal, or perhaps it's simply showing up for your next workout. Whatever it is, I encourage you to take that step with confidence, knowing that you have the knowledge, tools, and determination to succeed.

And with that, I'm not saying goodbye, but rather, see you later! I hope you'll carry these lessons with you, not just in your workouts, but in your daily life. And remember, no matter where you are in your fitness journey, you're stronger than you think. So, here's to you, your strength, and the incredible journey ahead. Keep lifting, keep growing, and keep shining!

If you want to find me online, I am active on my Instagram account, and I'd love to connect with you! @amynealcoaching is my handle. I will be there giving more workout movements and just fun motivation on your fitness journey. You can also find me on Facebook at Amy Neal Coaching.

Thanks for reading and I can't wait to hear from you!

Thank you for reading Strength Training For Women Over 40: Dumbbell Edition

If you enjoyed this book, I'd appreciate it
if you'd leave a review on Amazon!

Reviews help independent writers like me
get my book into the hands of more people like you!

Scan this QR code from your smartphone,
and it will take you directly to my book's review page!

I have also provided a live link that will take you directly to my review page! If you are reading from a device, click the link below!

https://www.amazon.com/review/create-review
/?ie=UTF8&channel=glance-detail&asin=B0D8ZNMQKS

Thank you again for reading my book. Stay strong and healthy!

References

1. McCall, P. (2015). Strength Training Improves Body Image and Physical ... *PubMed Central*. https://www.ncbi.nlm.nih.gov/pmc/articles/PMC4354895/

2. Gascoigne, T. (n.d.). Your Guide to Female Hormones and the Muscular ... *BOXROX*. https://www.boxrox.com/hormones-and-muscular-potential-of-women/

3. Schumann, L. (2010). Strength training for women: debunking myths that block ... *PubMed*. https://pubmed.ncbi.nlm.nih.gov/20086816/

4. Whole Health. (n.d.). The Difference between Body Weight and Body Composition. *Whole Health*. https://wholehealth.com/blogs/health/body-weight-and-body-composition-whats-the-difference

5. Rodriguez, N. (2018). Recent Perspectives Regarding the Role of Dietary Protein ... *PubMed Central*. https://www.ncbi.nlm.nih.gov/pmc/articles/PMC5852756/

6. Lanza, I. R., & Nair, K. S. (2009). Muscle tissue changes with aging. *PubMed Central*. https://www.ncbi.nlm.nih.gov/pmc/articles/PMC2804956/

7. Cava, E., & Strigini, F. A. L. (2020). Impact of Skeletal Muscle Mass on Metabolic Health. *PubMed Central*. https://www.ncbi.nlm.nih.gov/pmc/articles/PMC7090295/

8. Reynolds, G. (2023, January 3). What Is the Right Balance of Strength Training to Cardio? *The New York Times*. https://www.nytimes.com/2023/01/03/well/move/strength-training-cardio-exercise.html

9.   Aledbetter, J. (n.d.). 8 Benefits of Dumbbell Workouts for Women. *Julie Aledbetter*. https://www.juliealedbetter.com/ embrace-your-real/8-benefits-of-dumbbell-workouts-for-women

10. Torokhtiy, A. (n.d.). 12 Different Types of Dumbbells: The Ultimate Guide. *Torokhtiy*. https://torokhtiy.com/blogs/guides/types-of-dumbbells

11. GymGear. (n.d.). Safety First: How to Avoid Common Dumbbell Injuries. *GymGear*. https://gymgear.com/ safety-first-how-to-avoid-common-dumbbell-injuries/

12. Wikihow. (n.d.). How to Choose the Right Dumbbell Weight. *Wikihow*. https:// www.wikihow.com/Choose-the-Right-Dumbbell-Weight

13. WellTech. (n.d.). 8 Beginner Dumbbell Exercises (Build an Easy Full-Body ... *WellTech*. https://welltech.com/ content/8-beginner-dumbbell-exercises-build-an-easy-full-body-workout/

14. Slater, G. J., & Phillips, S. M. (2009). Nutritional aspects of women strength athletes. *PubMed Central*. https://www.ncbi.nlm.nih.gov/pmc/articles/PMC2564387/

15. Garage Gym Reviews. (2023). 19 Best Dumbbell Exercises for Building Muscle. *Garage Gym Reviews*. https://www.garagegymreviews.com/ best-dumbbell-exercises

16. Aaptiv. (n.d.). 6 Best Ways to Track Strength Training Progress. *Aaptiv*. https:// aaptiv.com/magazine/track-strength-progress/

17. Ace Fitness. (n.d.). 5 Benefits of Dumbbell Training. *Ace Fitness*. https://www.acefitness.org/resources/pros/ expert-articles/5675/5-benefits-of-dumbbell-training/

18. Fitbod. (n.d.). Full Body Dumbbell Workout (3 Examples). *Fitbod*. https:// fitbod.me/blog/full-body-dumbbell-workout/

19. Issa Online. (n.d.). How to Track Strength Training Progress for Better Results. *Issa Online*. https://www.issaonline.com/blog/post/ how-to-track-strength-training-progress-for-better-results

20. Hafstad, A. D., & Board, D. J. (2022). Evidence-Based Effects of High-Intensity Interval Training. *PubMed Central*. https://www.ncbi.nlm.nih.gov/pmc/articles/ PMC8294064/

21. FitnessBlender. (n.d.). 30 Minute Full Body Dumbbell Workout NO REPEAT (Advanced). *YouTube*. https://www.youtube.com/watch?v=4sUGg9mcMGU

22. APA Sport. (n.d.). Psychological Benefits of Exercise. *APA Sport*. https://appliedsportpsych.org/resources/health-fitness-resources/psychological-benefits-of-exercise/

23. Townsend, J. (n.d.). Sports Nutrition Part 2: Macronutrients & Micronutrients. *Integrative Medicine Center*. https://imcwc.com/sports-and-nutrition-part-2macronutrients-micronutrients/

24. Barbend. (n.d.). Your Ultimate Guide to Pre- and Post-Workout Nutrition. *Barbend*. https://barbend.com/pre-and-post-workout-nutrition/

25. Cullen, J. (2023). Hydration to Maximize Performance and Recovery. *PubMed Central*. https://www.ncbi.nlm.nih.gov/pmc/articles/PMC8336541/

26. NutriMeals. (n.d.). The Ultimate Guide to Meal Prep for Fitness and Muscle Gain. *NutriMeals*. https://nutrimeals.ca/blogs/news/the-ultimate-guide-to-meal-prep-for-fitness-and-muscle-gain

27. Krieger, J. W., & Stickley, C. D. (2014). Study: Consistency in Strength Training Matters More Than ... *Bicycling*. https://www.bicycling.com/training/a44641104/strength-training-consistency-study/

28. Fullagar, H. H. K., & Duffield, R. (2011). Sleep and muscle recovery: endocrinological and ... *PubMed*. https://pubmed.ncbi.nlm.nih.gov/21550729/

29. Alderman, L., & Landers, D. (2013). The Effects of Stress on Physical Activity and Exercise. *PubMed Central*. https://www.ncbi.nlm.nih.gov/pmc/articles/PMC3894304/

30. Healthline. (n.d.). Exercise Rest Day: Benefits, Importance, Tips, and More. *Healthline*. https://www.healthline.com/health/exercise-fitness/rest-day

31. Ace Fitness. (n.d.). 8 Time Management Tips to Help You Achieve Your Health ... *Ace Fitness*. https://www.acefitness.org/resources/everyone/blog/5454/8-time-management-tips-to-help-you-achieve-your-health-and-fitness-goals/

32. Verywell Fit. (n.d.). 6 Ways to Get Past a Weightlifting Plateau. *Verywell Fit*. https://www.verywellfit.com/six-tips-to-break-through-strength-training-plateaus-3120744

33. WebMD. (n.d.). Workout Injuries: Prevention and Treatment. *WebMD*. https://www.webmd.com/fitness-exercise/workout-injuries-prevention-and-treatment

34. Men's Health. (n.d.). 10 Evidence-backed Ways to Get Motivated to Work Out. *Men's Health*. https://www.menshealth.com/uk/building-muscle/a750272/5-ways-to-motivate-yourself-to-work-out/

Printed in Great Britain
by Amazon

46688534R00086